Images of Being There

Dean C. Gardner

ISBN 978-1-957956-14-5 (Paperback)
ISBN 978-1-957956-15-2 (Ebook)

Inquiries and Book Orders
should be addressed to:

Leavitt Peak Press
17901 Pioneer Blvd Ste L #298,
Artesia, California 90701
Phone #: 2092191548

SECTION 1:

times and a half

So
There is more
Than the here and now.

It is
That altered consciousness
Experiences paradigms
That do not
Conform to phenomenal reality.

There are realms and kingdoms
Of realms that exist
And they defy
The rational and reasonable
With their physics
Grounded
In the shadows
Of being toward Truth.

They are
As much of what
Is there
As the close at hand.

These places are
The source of ideation.

For the artist
The portal that links him in
Is accessed through the crystal crow
And the substance

Of the crystal crow.

Linear time
Has no bearing
To these places
As the celestial clocks
Rule the interlude
As mind belongs
To being outside
Of the body.

In these domains
Being in nothingness
Conform to the rubric
Of possibility
Where the mind loses
Contact
With the here and now
But is anchored
In the milestones
Of the other.

So
The artist visits there
To capture images
Of hidden meaning
And he is guided
By the substance
Of the crystal crow

A muse of sorts.

Through his inner eye
The artist
Penetrates the unknown
And the secrets
Of cosmic consciousness
Appear with the close
At hand.

Reaching
Beyond himself
He maps the way
To the authentic article
As he walks
Through a grave yard
The tombstones
Mirroring eternity.

It is
That what is there
Throws away
The masks
That hide Truth
And the artist
Gathers images
From the unknown.

Along the way

A seed drifts by
And the artist
Brings it to life.

Planted in his mind
The seed grows
Into a tall tree
Where birds nest
As time and times
And a half
Feed the interlude.

There is
A peculiar silence
To the moment
And the graves open.

Then
A trumpet sounds
And the bodies
Emerge whole and healthy
As they dance.

In the wind
Alleluias rise.

*

Through his inner eye
The old man
Sat in his garden

Watching the sunflowers
As if they were
Carnivorous beasts
Intent on devouring
The next moment.

Keeping his distance
He listened to their low growl
Ferociously hungry
As their shadows
Cast power in their stand.

Then
Angels sat beside him
And they talked
Of the deep sky
Cast in turquois
With clouds
Of a rich orange.

There was the fragrance
Of wonder
In the breeze
As the angels
Discussed the next painting.

Two gold rings
Perpendicular to each other
Were in the background
As well as a green and red
Figure running

From left to right
And another seated
In the background.

As the old artist
Looked into the earth
He saw time pass
Into an image of Truth.

Then his muse
Darted behind a rose bush
Laughing with good cheer
As she became
A whisper in the wind
And her mysterious ways
Fascinated the old man.

She was
His muse for decades
And decades
Inspiring him to witness
Being in time.

How he adored her
And her play
And she found worth
In his being toward Truth.

*

While in deep meditation
The artist saw
A string of pearls
Separated by a deep darkness
Each pearl
A moment linked
By nothingness.

Held in place
By the will
Of the thing itself
The pearls swirled
Through an amber mix.

How death
Stalks in circles
Feeding on dreams
Of the authentic article.

Space to the artist
Was a woven wonder
To feel in the heart
And look through what was there
To the substance of the thing
Itself.

He would take a thread
Of color
And configure it
To be something
An object of beauty

And meaning.

His struggle endured
Across his life
As demons intended
His demise
Ever trying to corrupt
His being
As he clungs to his faith
In The Unknown God.

The artist's muse
Was a golden chalice
A female filled
With tantalizing elixirs
Rich in fragrance
And filled with passion.

They were together
In half times as times
Unfolded
Into a dance of wonder
As she was the fabric
Of his dreams.

There were
Shapes and forms
To the geometry
Of his life
And he planted
Substance along the way

In colors
Vibrant with life
As his muse
Sang being toward Truth
Into light.

She was a song
And she was a dance
But more than that
She brought life
To his heart
A steady rhythm
Onto forevermore.

His muse
Was the music
Of his art.

*

With a dense fog
Covering the ridges
With an impenetrable gray
What was of the close
At hand appeared.

It was
A small universe
As the concealed
Emitted the sound
Of a train

Leaving no trace
Once it passed.

Angels spoke to the artist
About promise
And he drank in
Their message.

The artist saw
The mechanism of being toward Truth
As he took his brush
In hand
And he drew a line
Separating being in nothingness
Extending into the gray.

With the angels
Holding his hand steady
He plotted the figures
Of a multitude
Kneeling
Before The Word
And the canvas
Became alive
Vivid in its portrayal
Of a moment to be.

What he saw
Through his inner eye
He fashioned
In oils

As his muse rested
In the warmth
Of his heart.

He knew her look
And he understood
Her smile.

She was
His touchstone
To the beyond.

Their love
Magnified the quest
For The Spirit of Truth.

In a gray universe
They held a rainbow
In their hearts.

*

As angels dine
In the garden of possibility
Demons lurk in the shadows
Waiting for the chance
To seize control and power.

The angels are equipped
With the power
Of The Unknown God

While the demons
Are armed with machetes.

A battle ensues
With blood shed
Upon the garden
The Shasta daisies
Splattered with blood.

With the muse
By his side
The artist paints
The demons
And their carnage
Is filled with maggots.

What courage in the hands
Of righteousness
As he colors
The killing field.

Evil seeks power
While good offers peace.

With no end in sight
The demons inflicted wounds
Deep in the core
And some of the free
And brave lie devoid of life.

How the heart pounds
A strong rhythm
Of respect
For those heroes
Lost in combat.

At dusk
A bugle sounds taps
Followed by bagpipes
Singing Amazing Grace.

So
The war of principalities
Continues.

So
Truth claims victory
Once again
And the artist and muse
Carry on, together.

*

Searching
Through the expanse
Of being in nothingness
For the authentic article
The artist found
What was
The thing itself
In being toward Truth.

First, substance appeared
As an amorphous body
Altered
By the winds of eternity.

It was colors
Inside of colors
Changing
From the reds and the blacks
To blue and white
As a bolt of light
Shimmered through
In hunter green.

Next
A pyramid formed
From what was there
And it glowed
With an amber hue.

So
The substance
Consumed the here and now
As the pyramid grew
Into the beyond
And the sound
Of a heavy rain pounded
Into an absence
In the moment
A type of despair
That forced nothingness

Into the mind.

Then
The image vanished
While the feeling lingered.

As being toward Truth
Advanced from the beginning
Time and space thundered
Placing the concealed
Into a drift of thingness.

Then
The muse lit a candle
And placed it
On the artist's head.

Filling all that he was
With love
She pointed to a doorway
That led
To the authentic article.

Then
The muse placed
A smile
In his heart.

*

The bells chime
Seven times
And the hour marks
Quiet to the mind
As the muse emanates
What matters.

Out there rumbles
Time past
As echoes through eternity.

All along the way
The Unknown God
Held the artist
In hands of mercy
Because of his faith
And he walked
Onto destiny loaded
With images.

Once
With a friend
He climbed the cliffs
Outside Souix St. Marie
Ontario
And there was
A moment
When he should have
But he didn't.

The muse caught him.

Approaching the summit
He held onto a limb
Growing from a crack
In the stone facia.

It gave way
And somehow
He was caught
By the grace of The Word
As the muse brings
A melody to the now.

Visiting time past
The artist drew
A mountain suspended
In time and space
And at its top
Was a pyramid
With a seeing eye.

There were no clouds
No wind and the air was
Was pure.

How death
Warmed over by destiny
Configures being toward Truth
With the authentic article
And the muse delights
The artist
With a song of beauty.

Then she danced.

She is
His touchstone
To being toward Truth
His voice
Through light in the darkness.

She is
Of the here and now
And the distant beyond.

*

As her inner eye
Brought visions into the mind
Of the artist
His conscious left
His body
And she guided him
To a portal
Into the authentic article.

There
In the moment
Of transcendence
The mechanism of apprehending
The thing in itself
Exploded
Into the mystery
Of what matters most.

Times and times and a half
The complete history
Of the universe
Dissolved
Into a bead of light
As the muse shuffled
Being in nothingness.

Then
A golden wheat field
Dropped in
As a strong wind
Turned the scene
Into waves of silence.

Against the wind
The crystal crow struggled
To traverse
The expanse.

The going was slow.

A Cyprus tree
Bent in the furry
Of the moment
Was buffeted
By the invisible.

As the muse
Opened the eyes
Of the artist, he saw a stream

Of despair dance
Upon his heart but she fed him
With purpose
As she rose above
The interlude.

So
The Word had
Delivered hope

*

As his meditation
Took him
Into other dimensions
The artist saw
What was meant
By being toward Truth
At the threshold
Of the authentic article.

His muse offered him
A portal to the beyond
And she laid
Before him the wonders
Of what matters.

It was
The here and now
In the close at hand
That brought a shift

To his vision
Focusing on his star gate
With the muse.

She was
Of the here and now
And of the beyond
As he believed his way
To serve his muse
With the vision
Of hidden meaning revealed.

Dwelling
For the moment
In the subconscious
He traced the flight
Of being
Across multiple realities
And she triggered
Being in nothingness
In his mind.

In the face of despair
He held hope
In his heart
And she eclipsed
Nothingness
With purpose
And the love of another.

To touch
The image of her splendor
Brought him
A view
Of time and space
That transcended all
And everything
Until he was
In his mansion in the house
Of The Unknown God.

It was all
The workings
Of The Spirit of Truth.

*

Onto another horizon
The way of the wind
And purpose
Formed in clouds of space
The artist beheld
A butchered bull
Hanging on hooks.

In mass
It was startling
A thing
Of grotesque power
Drained
Of its blood.

It looked
More terrifying
As it was
Than what it had
Looked like
In life.

How
The look of death
Overpowers life.

How
The wounds
Of being toward Truth
Speak
From what matters.

Then
The artist fell
Into the wilderness
Of the here and now.

The landscape
Covered with a forest
Spoke
Into the reaches of mind
As the muse planted
A song
In the moment.

Then
The face
Of the crucified
Riddled
Times and a half
And the muse
Raised an anthem
Praising the innocence
Of The Word.

How
In history
Savage hearts devour
The flesh of the living.

*

At sunrise
Out of the east
Came crow after crow
To pay tribute
To the night's carnage.

On a mound
Alongside being toward Truth
A killdeer ran free
A witness
To the passion of times.

A ghost
Of the moon

Faded into the west
Its silence a testament
To the holding
Of the tongue.

On the ground
A measure of dew
Awoke blood
In the earth
And bodies emerged
From their resting place.

Then
A thick ichor
Oozed
Out of the forest
Smelling of life
Spent in darkness.

That morning
The muse washed
The stains
Of being in time
And the artist
Framed the image
Of what matters.

How powerful
The movement
Of space into form
And the artist

Painted
The moment in vivid colors.

Then
A screech from the depths
Broke through the air
As Truth
Rumbled through being toward Truth.

So
The artist advanced
Into the unknown
And the muse
Steadied his course
To eternity.

So
The morning spoke
Through the wonder
Of The Unknown God.

*

Across the vast native planes
The spirit of freedom lives
In the heart beat of the mustang.

They gallop from sunrise
To sunset
Declaring liberty
To ears that listen.

What power they bring
To the land
As the soul of natives
Rise in joy
As the mustang leaves
The signature
Of awesome symmetry.

In their muscle
And bone
In the very blood
Of their being
Lives the substance
Of what matters.

How
They sing of the land
Of the free and brave.

The song
Of the mustang
Carries the spirit
Of forevermore.

So vast
Their vision beckoning
Life and liberty
Before them
Yet
There are those
Who cut them down

Spilling their blood
Onto the land.

There are men
With no light
In their eyes
That take away
The freedom known
To the land.

They butcher
The mustang
But their spirit rises
Into the clouds.

They betray the Truth
Of freedom
Yet
The mustang lives on.

*

As the summer sun
Warms the back
The inner eye
Of the muse fastens
A look
To the here and now
Searching
For the concealed
And hidden meaning.

So
Within a forest
Of dreams life gathers
In the back of mind
And the artist
Seizes an image.

It is
Of a body
Hanging by its hands
Chained
To the invisible
As birds nest
In its long hair.

From somewhere
Comes
The beating of a drum
Pounding thunder
Into flesh.

Then
The artist mounts
His muscle and iron
Passing through
What is there onto eternity
As his mind
Configures the moment.

Taken
By The Spirit of Truth

The muse launches
Into the membranes
Of time and space
As the artist
Rolls
Down the road
To possibility.

Stopping
At the intersection
Of being in nothingness
The artist pictures
The moment as the sound
Of a distant crow
In flames.

Then
As the muse climbs
Golgatha
The world stops
And New Jerusalem
Rises from ashes.

*

In all the world
Only the sound
Of crows
Guarding the way
To Truth and life.

How massive the quiet
Of the hour.

In a moment
Of solitude
The artist pictures
The day
Before time
Where substance flows
Through what matters
Into a river of the beyond.

Time
Finds its place
In the beginning
As the movement
Of a river
Echoes the massiveness
Of being toward Truth.

Then
Within the fabric
Of being
The muse opens
The day
With first light
As the smell
Of the earth fills
What is there.

A sweet lullaby brings
Deliverance
Into the now
And the artist colors it
With sweet dreams.

So
The mind sings
In the hollows of the wilds
And the crystal crows allow
Entrance into the light
Of Truth.

Then
The geometry
Of being toward Truth defines
The passion
That brings life
Into the light
And the crystal crows feed
Off of the moment.

*

As angels gather
In the garden of tables and chairs
The muse sings beauty
Into the moment.

Peace covers them
With a wondrous glow

And the artist
Captures a picture
Of what is there.

In the foreground
Is a pond
Rich in lily pads
The blossoms
A lovely, pure white.

Dragon flies stir
The air
And the artist
Configures
The here and now
With a gentle persuasion
Toward the authentic article.

Forming negative space
The artist
Shadows of trees
Their branches
Swaying in the breeze.

Then
The muse raises
The day
Into a brilliant light
And the artist
Paints a portal to the beyond
Near the center

Of the pond
Where catfish come up
To pronounce
The peace beyond
Understanding.

It is
A moment
With The Spirit of Truth
As dreams fill
The artist
With vibrations
Of the forevermore.

How
Genuine the feel
Of being with The Word.

*

On the roadside
A carcass
That never saw
It coming
And the buck
Filled with maggots.

The artist
Turns to the muse
And she plants
Hidden meaning

In his brain.

How all life
Is destined for death
With each day lived
A gift.

Above
Vultures circling
And dinner
Waiting for guests.

In the heat
Of a summer's day
Time stops for a while
And images gather
In the corners
Of the mind.

Then
He charts
The coming and going
Of life
When only death
Is visible.

How
Time lasts for a while
And then it is
No more.

The unknown grows
More than time
As the vultures
Feast.

Times
And times and a half
Collect remnants
Of being toward Truth
Although time present
Overshadows the moment.

How
The road seems
Endless
As life goes on and on
And the muse
Colors the moment
With blood
As the artist pictures
The kill.

*

Being toward Truth
Where all that matters
Clusters
In the close at hand
Yet
Time conceals it
With a blind eye.

To approach this enigma
The artist calls
Upon the muse to clear
The air
And erase the shadows.

Then
The crystal crow lands
On his shoulder
Whispering secrets
About the always already there.
A brilliant light
Engulfs what is there
As hidden meaning
Rises into view.

So
The Spirit of Truth
Opens the inner eye
Allowing passage
Into the way, the Truth
And the life.

How
The faint heart
Steadies
Into a rhythm founded
Upon native drums
And the artist
Seizes
The authentic article

As time and space
Conforms
To the message of The Word.

How
Being in nothingness
Penetrates
The close at hand
And the inner eye views
Thoughts
Of The Unknown God.

How
Creation reveals
The coming and going
Of all that matters
As the promise
To being toward Truth
Rolls through the mind
And the crystal crow
Fills barrenness
With paths of wonder.

*

Upon the frontier
Of mind
Images rise
And the artist
Follows the dominos
Of being in time.

Leading the way
They bring
Wave after wave
Of what matters, as the muse
Searches
For the portal
To the other side
Of illusion.

Then
A cathedral emerges
Shimmering
As light passes by.

There are
No people there
Yet
The city glows
In its architecture.

Pigeons
Swarm in the portico
Taking flight
Alarmed by the sounding
Of bells.

Then
A thunderstorm
Breaks loose
And the sky carries
Darkness.

Lightning.

Thunder.

The rain is heavy
As the wind
Rushes by
Headed for the ends
Of the earth
While the cathedral bells
Continue their business.

As the muse
Gathers what matters
Where time present
Redeems time past
For time future
Followed by a look
Into vertical time
How truly
The dominos
Place one milestone
After another.

So
Connectivity is not
An illusion
After all.

*

Ever deeper into trance
The artist probed
The unknown parts of mind
As the muse crashed
Through dimension
After dimension
With The Spirit of Truth
Guiding her way.

It was
All a mystery
Of being in nothingness
As times unwound
Into a parabola of time
And the artist
Flirted
With the authentic article.

There were
Wheels inside of wheels
And a stretching
Of time and space
That opened a portal
To what matters.

The faces
Of a family of three
Potato eaters by blood
Sat at a table
With angels
Carrying the light

Of eternity
Above the daughter.

Mother and father
Wore years and years
Of hard work
And earth tones
Surrounded their life
Together.

How
Hard work defines
Character

As the next generation
Makes its way
Through the clutter
Of a mad, mad world
And a child
Wears innocence
In her look.

What carries them
Through their life
Is a faith
As their foundation
The cornerstone
Of being toward Truth.

To believe
In The Word brings

The power to endure
The oppression
Of the dull round.

*

In the back
Of mind
The crystal crow awakens being toward Truth
As the muse turns
The lights on
In the mind of the artist.

Alert in the moment
After exploring
Time and space, the artist
Left his trance
For the here and now.

A faint purple haze

Covered
The mountain ridges
As traffic rolled by.

It is
The urban rush
With somewhere to go
Pushing life
Into want and need
As the mustangs

Are slaughtered.

How
They are a symbol
Of freedom
Those mustangs
That belong to being toward Truth.

Howe
The mustangs roam
Across the expanse
With no owner except
The sky.

To see a herd
Brings breath to the spirit
As their romp speaks
Into a time

Of everlasting
Yet
They are slaughtered
In mass.

So
Freedom is murdered
As blood flows
In rivers
And urban man takes
No notice.

The artist paints
A scene
And it is a tragedy
Where the urban rush
Forgets
The as
The authentic article.

*

As the corner
Of the inner eye
Of the muse
Catches a glimpse
Of demons and their shadows
The ghosts
The artist calls
Upon The Spirit of Truth
For the powers
To overcome this evil.

Overhead
A hawk glides by
As a breeze
Unfolds being toward Truth.

The muse gathers
Angels
To fight the war
Of principalities
And The Word

Shields
This time and space.

How
The full armor
Of The Unknown God
Protects believers
From the ways
Of depravity
As the artist holds
His faith
Ever so closely.

The demons launch
Their assault
And the ghosts
Riddle the moment
With doubt
But the angels swarm
Upon them.

Then
This evil asks
To not be sent back
Into the lake of fire
And The Word
Turns the demons
Into a herd of pigs.

They run down a hill
To a river

And there they drown.

The ghosts
Follow with them
And are consumed
By the waters
Of faith and hope
As a hawk looks on
From on high.

*

The land
Belongs to the grandkids
And their children
As age
Invades the artist
And the muse embraces
Them
As a treasure
Onto everlasting.

So
The crystal crows know
The life of liberty
And from a watchful eye
They look onto times
And times and a half.

In the belly
Of being toward Truth

The sustenance
Of what matters trumps
The aches and pains
Acquired in a long time
As the crystal crows point
To the center
Of the universe.

It is
Faith that carries
Life
From one age
To another
As he heart accepts
That
Which is larger than self
And the artist
Carves meaning
Into life.

It is
A statue of love
That transcends the moment
As the muse guides
The artist
Onto picturing a statue
Of an older artist
Among the days
Of the here and now.

Then
The children of today
Inherit
A life of beautiful dreams
Surrounding the timeless
As the crystal crows
Look to faith
Onto one generation
And another
Onto forevermore.

The call of freedom
Is in the blood
Of a nation that preserves
Liberty.

Freedom
Without faith
Is dead.

SECTION 2:

the minute particular

The lake, calm
The wind gone
How the water reflects
Being in time
As the mind drifts
Across the mountain ridges.

The crystal crow, distant
Tells the moment
Into being toward Truth
And thoughts
Empty
Into time and space.

There is
A tree at the top
Of one more hill
Horizons
And horizons away
More distant now that time
Has taken its toll
And the artist
Plants a tree in the center
Of the universe.

To touch this tree
After a walk into the everlasting
Brings tears
And the memory of times of youth.

Then
The muse covers
The artist with kisses
Awakening his painting
Of lost love
The love of being
In the wilderness.

Then
One crow
And another and another
Carry
The moment
Into the blood of being toward Truth.

A great blue heron
Lands before
Mind
And his inner eye
Pierces
Time and space
As the muse pyramids
Into what matters.

There is
A freedom
In the wilderness
That enriches the blood.

How
the artist grows

Old?

*

A chorus of crows
Awakens times
As the past speaks
Of a sad story.

There is
A cradle, empty
Of life
And an old black dog
With head bowed
Before it.

It is
Years and years ago
That this image
Stirred the mind
Of the artist
As he paints
A geometry of sadness
Into the soul.

In the time
Of invincibility
Death took the heart
Of what mattered
Pulling life into despair.

How
To mourn the loss
Seems evident
In the somber tones
Of this image.

Grief and grieving.

Then
The muse carries
The eye
To a window
Opened to a steady breeze
As angels surround
What is there.

A lamp is lit
Over the cradle
Showering the moment
With the way
Through the grief
As the crystal crow stands
In the open window.

The artist turns
To the muse
And she guides him
Into the portrayal
Of an infant
Gone
Witnessed by an old

Black dog.

The family is
At the infant's funeral
And the crystal crow
Watches over the moment.

*

The canvas
Bare
Awakens dreams of a portal
To what is there
As the mind of the artist
Basks in the light
Of becoming.

There is
An image floating
In the back of being toward Truth
Escapes understanding
Yet
It is an image
That reaches into the substance
Of what matters.

A struggle emerges
Between figure and negative space
Between foreground
And background
As the muse

Clears
The message
Into discreet thoughts.

A stroke of light
Descending
From upper left
To lower right
Brings the nuance
Of energy
As form and substance
Swirls into place.

It is
Neither portrait nor landscape
But rather the joining
Of energies
With the mechanics
Of the authentic article.

A ring of gold
With oranges and greens
Displaces thought
As it becomes
A hallo
Passing onto a generation
Of dreams.

Within a triangle
There is an eye
And it fastens itself

In the middle of the ring.

Clouds pass over
The movement
As discernment makes
Meaning.

So
The symbols
Of being in nothingness
Emerge
Into a wondering
As the canvas exudes
A message far beyond
The close at hand.

*

Perhaps
The artform is dead
As the artist
Looks
Into what is there
And the muse
Weeps.

There is
A soldier standing by
As the crystal crow visits
With the authentic article
And time and space

Fill
With outliving self.

It is
The Unknown Soldier
Awakening
And the muse
Guides the artist
To the tomb.

On his knees
Crying out
To The Unknown God
The artist presses
Hidden meaning
Into the close at hand.

To approach Truth
The muse pulls
The artist
Out of death
And he takes his mind
Into what matters.

It is
His calling and solemn duty
To witness the moment
To reveal
The mystery of The Word
As life drives time and space
Into forevermore.

So
The hands grow numb
And the eyes blur
As thoughts
Color being toward Truth
With earth.

Then
The soldier salutes
The moment
And the crystal crow takes off
As the muse
Carries the artist
To where angels rest.

*

Some time back
There was
An elderly lady
Who mopped the floors
In a hospital.

It was
A time when the artist
First had an attachment
With crows.

No one paid
Attention to her
In this wonderland

Except the artist
Who revered her
For her labors.

Six days a week
She was there
Laboring for hours.

Her name is Alice.

The artist would
Sit by the windows
Early in the morning
And listen
To the crystal crows
While Allice mopped
The floors.

Cleaning the toilets
Was not beneath her
As her eyes sparkled
And her smile
Warmed being toward Truth.

There is
A special dignity
To manual labor
And there is
A certain freedom
Expressed in the call
Of crows.

It was
Alice who moved
The artist
To pay tribute
To a true lady
Earning her own way.

Captive of the moment
The artist turned
To his muse
Seeing a youthful Alice
A   woman
Who would not
Outlive herself
A spirit in touch
With the authentic article.

How
Freedom is
A state of mind
And a condition
Of the heart.

*

In the center
Of what is there
The crystal crow watched and waited
For the invasion
Of demonic entities
Ready to inflict

Havoc on being in time.

As thingness exuded
The thing in itself
Timer spun
Deep within silence
And the artist looked
To the muse
For understanding.

Image upon image
Ripped
Across the horizon
As the sky lit
With possibility
And the crystal crow
Eyed it all.

Then
The artist struck
The canvas
With a penetrating blue
As death breathed
Its last breath
And the muse formed
A figure
In time and space.

A certain knowledge
Of uncertain times
Took to the now

And the canvas
Became scarred
From wounds deep.

An angelic presence
Spreads wings of passion
And the muse
Appeared at the vortex
Of times and a half.

She glowed
As lady liberty, radiant
In the mix of things.

The muse bore the toll
Of war
With lightning
And bolts of fire
As demonic forces
Turned to rubble and ashes.

So
The crystal crow witnessed
The victory
Of freedom forevermore.

*

It is
Through the muse
That he enters the domain

Of the authentic article
Leaving behind
Outliving his self.

She gives him
The focus
Of being toward Truth
In the throws
Of a parabola of time.

She brings the dawn
Of what matters
As the artist attacks
Despair
With the will to be.

As her inner eye
Connects him
To the mystery
Of The Unknown God
She infuses him
With a destiny
Of righteousness.

Leaving the shadows
Of evil
The Word finds him
As The Spirit of Truth
Clears his mind
And purifies his heart.

It is
The muse
Through their loving bond
That he views
Hidden meaning
Painting the Truth
Of being toward Truth
And the crystal crow
As an escort takes him
To paradise lost.

How
The artist loves her
With all passion
In his blood
As he sees her in battle
With beasts.

With sword in hand
The muse carves out
The cruel oppressors
The evil and defiled
As the crystal crow
Carries the banner
Of paradise regained.

*

To view hidden meaning
The earth
Of the always already there

The muse undresses
Being in nothingness
As the crystal crow lifts the spirit
Of the artist.

There is
Life to the moment
As The Word
Speaks to the heart
Of being toward Truth.

Dancing
Upon the unconscious
The muse liberates
The concealed
As the artist opens
His being to a song
Of forevermore.

It is
That Truth cannot die
As the breath
Of what matters
Takes the artist
To new frontiers.

Then
Drums set the rhythm
To a gauntlet
Leading beyond space and time
As a trumpet sounds

And the muse takes the moment
Onto the sublime.

Leaving the close at hand
The artist ventures
Through a portal
In the mined
As being toward Truth steps
Into the authentic article.

There is
Meaning before words
As language enters song
And the cry
Of a blue jay touches
The inner most parts.

It is
The matter of faith
That speaks of freedom
As destiny brings
The embrace
Of an epiphany
And the will
Of The Unknown God
Feeds the muse
With loving kindness
With power and might
As the artist etches

What is there into being.

*

It is
A day when the ridges
Are filled with grandeur
When the forest
Is thick
With the call of the wild.

There is a certain
Freedom
Inherent in the wilderness
The freedom to think
And the freedom to be.

For the unknown
The artist holds respect
As times grow thick
With life
And the muse dances
In the mind.

Basking in the light
Of forevermore
A hawk dreams
Of the next meal
And the rabbit feeds
In shadows.

While eternity
Speaks to the heart
The mind seizes life
As time present
Walks on water, a miracle
Of what matters.

In this place
Visions surface
As the inner eye
Scans
The long and short
Of being toward Truth.

Then
The hawk takes
To wing
As the rabbit
Eats its last meal.

There is life and there is
Death
And both are unfathomable.

So
The philosophers attempt
To explain it all
While the artist draws
Pictures in the sand
And the hawk fills

Its belly.

*

In a universe
Of being toward Truth
Only the inner eye
Sees truth
As the shadows
On the cave wall
Point
To nothingness.

Leaving behind the illusions
Of linear time
The artist steps
Where the past and present
Are one
Looking to the future.

It is
The length and breadth
Of a parabola of time.

As the muse showers
This now point with promise
And being toward Truth
Proceeds to a milestone
The mind yearns
For a glimpse
At a vertical column of time.

Standing watch
The crystal crow answers the call
Of what matters
As free will takes flight
Behind being in time.

Somewhere
A legion of angels
Marches
Into the battle of history
As the objective self
Sees only darkness.

Then
The Spirit of Truth
Takes the moment
Through a gauntlet
To reality
As the muse conceals herself
And the artist weeps
In silence.

There is
A portal in the mind
That allows access
To the wonders
Of times and a half
But the dull round
Sees only nothingness.

So
The truth has evaded
Detection
As the muse
Discharged being toward Truth.

*

So
The earth is
Billions of years old
And the universe is
Billions and billions
Of years old.

Then
The big bang.

So
How many big bangs
Are there in eternity?

Then
There is the idea
That time slows down
When approaching
Th speed of light.

So
There is the cosmic clock
The celestial clock

And the biological clock.

So
The cosmic clock
Is a one-dimensional
Reality
And the celestial clock
Is a two-dimensional
Reality
And the biological clock
Is a three-dimensional
Reality.

Then
What evidence is there
That tells
Which of these clocks
Is affected
By approaching the speed
Of light?

So
The artist lives
According
To the biological clock
And his paintings are
According
To the celestial clock
As he dreams
According
To the cosmic clock.

So
The breath
Of flesh and bone and blood
Is governed
By the biological clock.

So
The artist lives
In a three-dimensional
Reality
And he paints
A two-dimensional
Reality
As the muse exists
In a one-dimensional
Reality.

So
What is the source
Of ideation?

*

As the mind digs deep
Into the earth
Of the always already there
Passion drives the moment
Toward a portal
Leading to what matters.

There is

A force within self
That seeks the substance
Of the unknown
And it infuses the will
With the power
To see hidden meaning.

To seek Truth
While the world
Lives in self-deception
How
The Spirit of Truth
Reveals
The way through the wilds.

What sweet treasure
Waits
For a leap of faith.

Then
The artist views
The canvas
As a departure
From the close at hand
To the beyond.

So
The portal opens
And the canvas fills
With forms
And images of forms

As The Word takes him
To his mansion
In the house
Of The Unknown God.

In this presence
The muse
Feeds the artist
The substance
Of being in time
As a light discloses
Dreams with deliverance.

The artist has seen
His dwelling
Onto forevermore
And vows to serve
The promise.

*

In the garden
Of tables and chairs
The horizon unfolds
Into a myriad of frontiers
And the artist sees
The light and shadows
Of the always already there.

How the roots
Of the forest pull

The earth
Through time and space
As the muse speaks
With angels
At the edge of the abyss.

So
Nothingness is as a void
An absence
Of time and space
A separation
From what matters
And for the mind
A place
That outlives self.

As the artist
Tightens his grip
On free will
He portrays a landscape
Infused with a reality
Beyond the frontiers
And into the heart
Of the mutual- dependence
Of being and being toward Truth.

Since what is
Is not sufficient
To disclose
What matters most
The muse takes

The vision of the artist
Onto a storehouse
Of treasures
Within forevermore.

There
He finds the beginning
Of hope
As angels minister
To his spirit
And the muse charts
The way
Across the expanse
Erasing the angst
Of nothingness.

Finding his way
Through the frontiers
Those gauntlets
Of being in time
Th artist embraces the muse
His treasure
In the here and now.

So
Nothingness
No longer exists
But language plays
In the garden
Of tables and chairs.

So
Nothingness
Is the disguise
Of self-deception.

*

When being communes
With being toward Truth
Things in themselves
Dance
As the other.

In that moment
Time and space
Become a language
And symbols
Of what matters
Unearthed
From the close at hand.

To touch
With the mind
The waters
Of the always already there
Pyramids
The substance
Of the deep
As free will surfaces
Upon a river of thoughts.

Then
A portal opens
To a looking glass
As images
Portray the self
And the artist
Consumes
Being in time.

The other is there.

Being is there.

So
The artist reaches
Into times
And times and a half
Stirring his mind
And the muse
As the other defines
An image
Outside phenomenal reality.

A ladder of gold
Presents itself
And the artist climbs
Out of himself
As the muse configures
A body of water
Where ideas swim.

Here
Dwells the origin
Of being and being toward Truth
A mystery
Of Truth
And the science of Truth.

How
The other as being
Sets boundaries
Of being toward Truth
The boundaries
Of the artist.

*

As wars
And rumors of war
Confound the moment
Freedom stands tall
And the stars and stripes
Serve and protect
All those who live
In freedom.

So
The world has grown
To the measure
Where tyranny and threats
Are obsolete.

Soon
It will become
The time
When whole masses
Of people vanish
When the lives
Of the lost
Are grieved.

Mass destruction is
No answer
Yet
Doom is inevitable.

How
The faces of all those
Who perish signal
The presence
Of a world gone mad.

When human life
No longer has value
And tyrants leverage
Power
The leaders
Of the free world
Must stand.

In the shadows
Of the moment, the artist
Paints the horror

Of nuclear war
The very instant
Of a blast.

What is there
No longer is there
As the smell
Of the carnage
Leaves no trace.

So
The muse weeps
And the artist wrings
His hands
Because there is
No longer a time for peace.

*

Through deep meditation
The artist connects
To the substance of being
And the always already there
As the muse
Fills being toward Truth
With things in themselves.

It is
A passing
Through phenomenal reality
And entrance

Through a gauntlet
Of times
And times and a half.

In the center
Of all and everything
Belongs the domain
Of the authentic article
And the presence
Of The Unknown God.

The power
Of the close at hand
No longer dictates
Perception
As time and space
Unite with the other.

Then
Just before the chasm
Of oblivion
The artist tastes life
And what matters
Free will
And freedom, itself.

How
The Spirit of Truth
Carries the artist
Into both peace and delight
As The Word

Welcomes the muse
Into paradise.

How
Believing in The Word
Brings a bounty
Of life
As the artist
Climbs outside himself.

It is not
An escape from reality
But a marriage
Of being in nothingness.

It is
Believing The Word
As the way, the truth
And the life.

I believe
Help Thou my unbelief.

*

Standing watch
At the top of the world
The crystal crow eyes the moment
As silence heaves
In the shadows.

There is
An instant
Before annihilation
That moves
Across the city
As the architecture
Of the last morning
Rises
From the horizon.

Then
The crystal crow leaves the scene
And the artist
Digs into the heart
Of the everlasting.

Seconds pass
And the call of the crystal crow
From somewhere else
Warns of the crash
Of time and space.

It is the end.

As the muse
Soars over what is there
The artist follows
The look of the crystal crow
And being in time
Stretches into eternity.

There
The artist moves
The canvas
Into a burst
Of the no longer
And the city turns
Into rubble.

Vaporized
Life there has
No place
As memories
Of a city on a hill
Seem like a dream.

Th muse
The crystal crow and the artist
Survive
The moment
As the vision
Of the lost melts
With the folly of men.

*

So
Three-dimensional reality
Forms linear time
And the biological clock
Depends upon it
As the beginning

Of time and space.

Then
The artist conceives
Life
As the everlasting.

Then
The muse dances
Out of the universe
And being
Separates from nothingness.

To the artist
It is the figure
That dances life
Into the moment
That celebrates Truth
As the rubric
Of what is there.

So
In the big bang
Life is there
As the dance
Continues
From the beginning.

There is no end
To forever
As being is forever

As all of life
Is always already there.

How
The conscious struggles
With death
Yet
It is the opening
To what matters.

Suddenly
The Spirit of Truth
Speaks
To the substance of being
And mankind awakens.

So
The earth is the center
Of theological activity
As faith defines
What matters most.

So
The Word offers the way
To The Unknown God.

*

To disassemble being
Until its original parts
Are in the close at hand

How
The whole
Exceeds thought
While the exposed parts
Alone
Mean dribble.

How
Being together
Advances
What matters
As the muse sings
An anthem of delight
And the artist
Steps
Back into self.

So
The truth of the inner
And the truth of the outer
Eclipse each other.

So
There is a tension
Of unknowns
And the muse forms
A divide
Of time and space.

A day in the life
Does not define

The who
Of being toward Truth.

As the artist
Moves
From one moment
To another
He captures a view
Not only what
Is there
But also the value
Of the mystery
Of being.

So
The muse precedes
The image
And she calls
Hidden meaning
Into form and substance.

How
The landscape
Of inner and outer
Universes
Fill the song
Of the muse with passion
And the artist receives
Her triumph

With joy and wonder.

*

On a park bench where the forest
Touches the heart
The artist writhes in thought.

Ideas
Drive the moment
As time and space
Release
The energy of being toward Truth.

Explosion

Apocalypse

Epiphany

Looking
Into the mechanism
Of phenomenal reality
The artist
Conceives the moment
As a step
Into hidden meaning.

Then
The Spirit of Truth
Takes his thought

Beneath pools
Of mystery.

He pulls together
His conscious
As his mind slowly
Unwinds
And the muse
Dresses his wounds.

Off in the distance
The sound of drums
Carries his heart
Into the rhythm of eternity
As his mind
Fixes upon this side
Of the other.

Then
Angels open his eyes
To the wonder
Of The Unknown God
And he fathoms
The expanse
As the always already there.

Embedded
In this moment
Is the promise
Of The Word
And the artist serves

This Truth.

*

In the garden
Of tables and chairs
A voice penetrates
What matters
With the power to move
Being into nothingness.

It is
The voice of an animal
Whining
In a moment
Of pain.

It is
The last cry
Of life
With the signature
Of dying.

How
That sound speaks
Light into shadows
As the artist
Paints
A roadside kill
And the crystal crow
Hungry looks on.

As the canvas
Bleeds.

With the carnage
A life
Gives up its last.

How pure
The sky that fills
With crystal blue
And the muse
Carries the image
Of loss.

To grieve over death
How the silence
After the last breath
Digs deep
Into the substance
Of being toward Truth
And the image
Of a young child
Carrying his dead puppy
Leaves a mark.

The body limp
The puppy
Leaves a trace
In a young boy's life.

How
This love never dies
But lives with the child
Forevermore.

*

It is
The little brown duck
Up from the bottom
Of the lake
With a smile
That moves thought
Into mountains and eons
Of possibility.

So
An ancient figure
Drafted this piece
And he composed
This poetic leap.

So
If ducks do not smile
Perhaps it was
The smile of the poet
At the thought
Of the incident.

The artist knows
That he cannot paint

The image
Because it is
A thought
Of another kind.

Portraying it
In full color
In the back of the artist's mind
Brings life
To the moment
As the artist
Becomes the other
In the close at hand.

It is
The poetic leap
That cannot be painted
And the dance
Of the muse
Surpasses the imagined.

To paint a picture
Is an idea
Figured
As a two-dimensional reality
While the poetic leap
Is pure ideation
And a one-dimensional
Reality.

It is the thought
Beyond the image
That lingers
Onto forevermore.

So
The artist cannot paint
The scene
Because of the mystery
Of the dance of the other.

*

Eclipsed
By the other
The artist finds
The negative space
Defining
The authentic article
As the pose
Of free will articulates
What matters.

It is
That each thought
Brings up an image
Surrounded
By the music
Of the always already
There.

Dancing on the edge
Of nothingness
The muse inhales
Life
And the mountains
Celebrate being toward Truth.

So
The flight
Of a hawk takes
The artist into circles
Of things in themselves
And time wears thin.

It is
That he feels the image
On the canvas
Has a will
All of its own
As the muse
Moves earth into his being.

There is
Meaning in the image
Far beyond himself
As he approaches
Nothingness.

Out of his being
Time and space
Grapple with the image

Portrayed in stillness.

How
His pain
Colors what is there
And the muse
Guides his hand
To uncover hidden meaning.

In this pose
He seizes an epiphany
Of times and a half
As the other frees him
Forevermore.

*

First light
And the dawn
Of eternity
Greet the inner eye
With awakening.

Out there
In the hands
Of time and space
The other rises
From the shadows.

Then
The artist captures

An image
Of hidden meaning
And the muse
Brings it to life.

It is
The look of a face
That sees
Beyond the here and now
A mask
Of being in nothingness.

Behind the mask
Is a vast water
Deep in mystery
As the inner eye
Searches
Through times and moments
Of times
Where history tells
Of the other.

So
There is the artist
Grown through linear time
And feeding
Upon the milestones
Set by the other
As the muse
Colors the face
With war paint.

There is power in his look.

There is dignity in his look.

How
This face represents
A people
Of wind and fire
As the artist
Bleeds with compassion.

So
This dawn
Is dedicated
To the free spirit
The other beyond being.

*

In the center
Of the inner eye
Glows a star
And it provides
Access
To worlds beyond worlds.

To listen
To the voice
Of hidden meaning
Unveils
Phenomenal reality

As the earth within mind.

There
Dwells the always
Already there
And the moment
Transcends time.

So
The self finds
The who of being
As the what
Of the other
Surrounds possibility.

All of the other
Is the reach
Of mind
As the artist
Forms a still life.

Then
The muse orchestrates
A tempest
That fills the sails
Of the conscious
With a passion
Of time and space
And the artist follows
The pigment of destiny.

As death closes
The eyes of life, the artist sees
The ground of becoming
And the muse
Naked in her time
Removes the mask
Of what is there.

Then
From the shadows
Of silence
The voice of the crystal crow
Calls to order what matters
As the artist paints
A portal
To the beyond.

So
The painting
Is that portal
Through the inner eye
And onto worlds beyond worlds.

*

In a day of darkness
A smile shines
The way
To a greater good.

Time slips away

Through the outstretched arms
Of the sleepwalker
As the muse poses
For the artist.

She
Beams with a glimmering gold
And her movements
Fluid
As the artist portrays her
In wondrous mystery.

On the canvas
There is no darkness
Because the artist
Sees
Through the eyes of love
Although the world spins
Chaos
Into the background
And the horizon
Quakes with madness.

So
She dances in waves
Of beauty
Revealing the good
Of the moment.

There is
A goodness

In her smile that transcends
Phenomenal reality
As the backdrop
Of the world grows
Ugly.

Suddenly
Music fills the moment
With the pounding
Of drums
And the voice
Of a flute
As the crystal crow lands
At her feet.

So
Free will
Takes a free spirit
Into what makes life
Worthwhile:
A smile of love.

*

In the shadows of mind
Demons
Twist thoughts
And are bent on destroying
All that matters.

Times and times ago

The artist toyed
With evil
And he lost his face.

Then
Came the time
When he repented
Searching for forgiveness
And finding it
In The Word.

What once was
Ugly
Became the beauty
Of a true mind
And a pure heart
Yet
He could not forget
His dance with evil.

Filled with The Spirit of Truth
He walked away
From his past
Finding hope through faith.

He learned the meaning
Of amazing grace
That rescued him
From torment
And from a lake of fire.

How
Belief in the power
And majesty
Of The Unknown God
Brought him
Onto a solid foundation.

Then
He was sent a muse
To partner with him
Upon an even path
And guard his spirit.

So
The artist
Began to learn
The way of Truth
In life.

*

So
The free spirit wears
The mask
Of the crystal crow
And all of being
Wants and needs time
To unsheathe the dagger
Of what matters.

Slicing through the quick
Of despair
Hope slaughters
Outliving oneself
As the weapon of defense
The authentic article
Bleeds forlornness dry.

There is
A union of spirits
That binds being
To being
While linear time
Assembles the experiential
Into destiny.

So
Destiny cannot be
Viewed
From the now
But only when one
Is outside of oneself
As the conscious
Pierces being toward Truth
With the blade
Of Truth.

Then
The crystal crow
Flies into the back
Of mind

And the artist
Unfolds realty
As entities
In the close at hand.

What is
Accessible in the moment
Is all of the unknown
And the ramparts
Of possibility
While the crystal crow
Defines the self
In terms of the limits
Of the experiential.

So
The free spirit
Beyond limitation
Dons the armor
Of a warrior
To fight the good fight
As the muse
Joins the crystal crow
In the always already there.

*

In a garden
Where angels sing
And the blossoms
Bloom in radiance

The artist chooses
To paint
Being and being toward Truth.

It is
That being
Comes from the beyond
And the always already there
While being toward Truth
Roots in the experiential
And the close at hand.

Through linear time
The biological clock
Unwinds toward death
While the cosmic clock
Grounds what matters
Into forevermore.

It is
The workings
Of the celestial clock
To chart destiny
And the muse dwells there
As a companion
In time and space.

How the garden
And the angels of the garden
Mirror the splendor
In the beyond.

How
The artist defines
The here and now
As a memory
In the moment
Of a parabola of time
And from there, the muse
Opens
A vertical column of time
To his being toward Truth.

So
Being is grounded
In a vertical column of time
While being toward Truth
Defines itself
In what it readily
Apprehends.

So
A parabola of time
Remains a portal
For being toward Truth
To seek
The wonders of being.

So
Being is an entity
While being toward Truth
Is a conscious force
That sets the boundaries

Of being.

*

An autumn chill
Awakens the mind
To times
And moments of time
As the muse
Embraces the artist
With the power
To understand.

In the image
On the canvas
A face draws near
As the light
Of another kind
Grows into Truth.

It is
Between the lips
That the concealed
Opens
To the wonders
Of possibility
The passage of the breath
Into life.

The nose is arched
And the eyebrows raised
As a question
Toward meaning
Identifies the other
As the muse pumps
What matters
In vibrant colors.

Then
In the spirit of things
The crystal crow touches the heart
And destiny
Sees free will
Manifest itself.

How
The moment overshadows
Time
As the image pulls life
Together
And the other
Undresses the secrets
In being toward Truth.

How
The image has
A will all its own.

How
The muse deciphers

The meaning
Behind the look.

It is
A face of questions
Opening the unknown.

*

Listening to the wind
The artist found
The majesty
Of The Unknown God
As the muse
Traced light through the wilds.

The trees speak
A language discernible
Through the inner eye
As time interjects
A portal to the beyond.

The mystery
Of hidden meaning
Inhabits
The far reaches
Of possibility
As the muse shadows
The moment.

Radiant
The sun tells
The story
Of life and death
As faith in The Word
Becomes
The starting point
Of eternity.

Then
The artist reads
The coming and going
Of time
As the muse
Rides the waves
Of wind.

To know nothing
Is
To not know anything
Because nothing
Does not exist
Except for expressing
Absence and despair
An emotional reality.

The wind defines
Being at the edge
Of an abyss
As a tirade of fire
Carries knowledge

To its valiant end
Yet
It is The Spirit of Truth
That stretches
The artist
Into the everlasting
And a place
Ever so amazing.

Possessing free will
The artist and muse
Dream their reality.

*

As the mind moves
From inner to outer
Substance shifts
To a two-dimensional reality
And the artist
Grows
Into the unknown.

It is
His world
That defines
What is there
And it is the other
That defines
What is not.

Mountains
Leaping into the sky
And the artist is dwarfed
By their presence.

Then
As the mountains
Form in the back
Of his mind
The muse grips him
And the mountains
Burst into flames.

His view carries him
Into the everlasting
Where the pulse
Of being touches
Moments of time
And the muse
Fills his cup
With a wild brew.

From the prison
Of mind
The artist seizes
What is there
And the muse
Issues his free will.

Then
The blue ridge mountains

Cry out for deliverance
As the muse
Reconfigures time and space.

So
Free will
Births the composition
As possibility
And dreams encompass
The landscape.

*

It was
His purpose to paint
Truth
The reality and the masks
Of reality
As he looked
Upon his composition
And the muse
Presented him
With a portal to the concealed.

How
Through the inner eye
Reality registers thingness
And things in themselves.

It is
A seeing in

And a seeing through
As a music
From within defines
The chatter
Of the without.

How
The image becomes
The gauntlet
That launches being
Into hidden meaning
As the sounds
of the drum and pipes
liquifies being toward Truth
and the muse
drinks deeply
the lifer of the artist.

In the sky
There is a doorway
That leads
To another side
Of what is there
Without the masks
And beyond time.

It is
Within moments
That Truth
Becomes apparent
And the artist records

Those life bearing
Moments.

How
The drums and pipe
Surround what is
As the heart
Finds a new rhythm
A rhythm grounded
In Truth.

*

So
Truth resides
Beyond and behind
The close at hand
As hidden meaning resides
Within the concealed.

There are
Masks and layers
Of masks
Covering what is
As the muse
Directs the artist
To see
Into the heart
Of being toward Truth.

It is
All in a moment
When the celestial clocks
Acknowledge free will
And the attempt
To see Truth.

The toll
Of bells marks
The time
When illusions disappear
As the artist rises
Over the mountains
And fades
Into the looking glass
Of being in time.

Juxtaposing
The moment
As a parabola of time
To the rule
Of the cosmic clock
Eternity moves the heart
Of reality
Into the clarity of the other
And the other views
The composition
With enlightenment.

Then
The other

Walks by in shadows
Of thought
And the muse
Finds a breath
Of life
Buried in the earth
Of becoming.

How
A moment of Truth
Connects the beyond
To what matters
As the artist forms
An epiphany
In time and space.

*

Looking through the mind
Th artist waits
For possibility
To show the way
Through a gauntlet
Of time and space
As the other
Leaves no trace
In the forbidden.

The muse is there
Hiding
Behind thoughts.

A stand of trees
Conceals the present.

It is
The search
For a true mind
Within his self
That brings life
Into a moment
Of memory.

There
Beneath the debris
Of absence
The muse pulls
The artist
Through the inner eye
And the stand
Of trees
Bursts into flames.

Then
The mystery
Of being toward Truth
With the authentic article
Emanates
From the gauntlet
And the artist
Sees himself
In a pure light
As images of possibility

Fill the unknown.

From one side
Of what is there
A hand stretches to touch a portal
While the muse ignites
Being in time with another vision.

So
The crystal crow knows
Truth
And the way to get there
As the artist
Turns to the wilds
For the elements of what matters.

*

How
The crystal crow calls beauty
From far away
To the moment
When life
Begins anew.

How
the sound of drums
infuses an energy
to look
into the vital.

So
Being toward Truth
And open to the wonders
Of the eternal
Allow access
To magnificence.

Then
The muse orchestrates
Beauty
Into the close at hand
As the crystal crow
Occupies the mind
And the artist
Portrays
The other side
Of nothingness.

As the artist
Speeds
Through a looking glass
He embraces the power
Of The Unknown God
And whole worlds
Emerge
From the unknown.

As The Word
Fills time and space
With the robust
The crystal crow

Introduces the mind
To the always already there.

Then
The muse rubs
Fire
Into the moment
As the artist blazes
A view
Of phenomenal reality
Unlike any other form.

So
The engine
Of all and everything
The Spirit of Truth
Powers
The song of beauty
Into the artist's touch.
on

*

The moon, full
Passes over the darkness
And a train heads
Into the unknown.

What matters makes
The earth tremble
As being toward Truth sees

Into mind
And the artist charges
Through the moment
When the moon
Summons
The ghosts of times past.

Angels come
To preserve and protect
The artist
And the muse
Follows their light
Across the night sky.

There
In silence
As an old man
Follows the unknown
Onto visions
Beyond being in nothingness.

Then
The ghosts
Filled with want
Drive the world
Toward chaos
As the angels guard
The heart from infamy.

How
Being toward Truth

Composing a portrait
Brings a time
When the unknown
Explodes into epiphany
But the ghosts
Of time past
Riddle the mind
With doubts.

How
The angels occupy
The heart
With power and might
As the mind struggles
In silence.

Then
The crystal crow brings manna
To being toward Truth
As the portrait lives
On and on.

*

Time is not
An illusion, but rather
A function
Of three clocks:
The biological clock
With linear time
The celestial clock

With a parabola of time
And the cosmic clock
With a vertical column
Of time.

Dwelling as a life form
Being toward Truth experiences
Linear time
Through consciousness
As time past, time present
And time future.

That
Which is not living
And exists
As time past
And time present.

That
Which is
Of another kind
Where pure ideation occurs
In the form of essence
Is the cosmic clock
A time
Of the always already there
A consciousness
Of the all-encompassing now
And the original source
Of consciousness.

The artist
Lives
In linear time
As a life form
With consciousness
Of the close at hand
While he paints
A two-dimensional reality.

His sculptures are
A mask
Concealing a two-dimensional
Reality
A mirror of the other
A shadow on a cave wall.

His muse
Is of the realm
Of essence
And the source
Of ideation
Grounded in the cosmic clock
A one-dimensional reality.

*

It is
That the boundaries
Of self
Are set by the other
While being toward Truth

Expands
In the close at hand.

It is
A rhythm
Of phenomenal reality
Where two energies
Mix
In the confluence
Of what is there.

When
A portal opens
These energies empower
Passage
Through a gauntlet
To the beyond
Rising to the level
Of a vertical column of time.

How
Pure magnificence
Resides there
Where no shadows
Of doubt intervene.

How
Blessed assurance
The authentic article
And things in themselves
Shine

As a staircase
Into unknown majesty.

Each step
Is a milestone
To eternity.

It is
Contact
With the Ultimate Other
The Unknown God.

The deeper the trance
The greater the energy
As self and being toward Truth
Form a boned
Of kindred spirits.

In this place
Nothing is concealed
And all of hidden meaning
Is grasped
As the close at hand.

It is
The power of The Word
That drives the engine
And it is fueled
By The Spirit of Truth.

*

Married
to

*

Married
To an art form
The artist touches
The voice
Of being toward Truth
As the muse
Consummates his vision.

There is
A wilderness in the look
Of the image
That dances
Out of his blood
As his heart pours life
Before the feet
Of the muse.

It is
A sculpture
Of being in time
Meeting a wasteland
Of one
Out living self
As the drums of eternity
pound
something into nothing.

How
The thought
Of the image
Calls into form
Being broken by grief
And the other
Holds the moment
Together.

So
The other
Is the image
And the image becomes
The infusion
Of despair.

How
Agony completes
The moment
As the artist folds
Pain into time.

Then
The children of hope
Take what is there
Into a terrain of dreams
And the artist
Offers a solitary scream
Among the tombstones

Of the living.

*

In the wilderness
Death is the matter that life feeds upon
As one day comes
And another goes as common place.

The mind
Grows accustom to time
Passing
And the hour
Of the unknown
Finds its posture
In a window
Where being toward Truth sees
Death everywhere.

What luxury it is
To be untouched by chaos
To be free
From the terror of war
And famine.

So
Whole cities cry out
With the blood
Of life
Flowing through the streets
And the mind looks

The other way.

So
A child soldier
Fires his weapon
Into the belly
Of the living, and the artist
Dances
With the love of the muse.

How
Mankind suffers
In countless ways
As the blood
Of humanity fills
The seas.

So
The artist paints
Pretty pictures
While bodies rot
Mutilated by hate.

So
Men, women and children
Starve in the muck
And the artist feels guilt.

To disconnect from the loss
When all owns the cause
Of the tragedies

How being toward Truth weeps
With grief.

*

A dense fog
Conceals the mountains
And the artist
Walks into clouds
As time moves
Toward end times.

It is
The celestial clocks
That coo
In the night
Speaking a language
Of time and space.

Through the inner eye
Hocus pocus disappears
Before the advance
Of mind
As being toward Truth
Navigates
From the known
To the unknown.

There are
Secrets in the sky

That whisper
In the wind
And the artist listens.

Then
The sky opens
To celestial dynasties
Where Truth
Resides
And the muse
Launches
Into their midst
To learn the ways
Of eternity.

Feeding
On dark matter
The artist embraces
Nothingness
And the muse finds
The encompassing
As the home
Of forevermore.

So
The fog conceals
What is there
And the artist
Sees
What is no longer
While the muse

Takes him into trance.

Then
Nothingness clings
To the mind
As being toward Truth grows
Into the unknown.

From theory to reality
The pursuit of knowledge
A dangerous thing.

✦

Where the inner world
Meets the outer
The conscious
Establishes being toward Truth
While the other stands
As phenomenal reality.

So
The real world
Meets the unreal
The architecture
Of the living
And Truth appears
As the unknown.

From the unconscious
To the subconscious

And preconscious
Self grapples with illusions
Although timer and space
Suggest an entrance
Into what is there.

Building upon the moment
The artist sees
Between being in nothingness
Choosing to depict
The tension
Between what is there
And what is not there.

How
The illusion
Of the real
Augments the apprehension
Of self
As dreams and hopes
Construct what is true.

Then
The muse ushers
Faith
Before the looking glass
Of the integrated collective
And the artist
Arranges the geometry
Of being in time
Into patterns of meaning.

So
It is by faith
That the mind trusts
The close at hand
And whole worlds
Beyond self
Open to a vision
Of what matters.

Braving the moment
Being toward Truth follows
The muse
Into the earth
Of the unknown
As the self
Reaches
For the Truth
Through faith
In something.

To have no faith
Is to be consumed
By despair.

SECTION 3:

beyond being
toward Truth

So
The artist was given
A true mind and a pure heart
And he wondered
What effect that would have
Upon his art.

Leaving the catacombs
Of time and space
He traversed oblivion
Where bodies drifted
Aimlessly.

In a back room
Of mind
A memory surfaced
Of a wealthy man
Gorging himself
On rich, tasty foods
While beneath his table
A poor man
Ate crumbs that had fallen
From the table.

Then
The poor man died
And lived on in the afterlife
With peace and joy.

Then
The rich man died

And he dwelt
In a lake of fire
For his afterlife.

The rich man called out
To have the poor man
Bring him a drop of water
For he thirsted.

There was a vast cavern
Between the rich man and poor man:
One that the poor man
Could not traverse

Then
The rich man asked
the poor man
to go and tell
his brothers
that the price for unbelief
was eternal suffering.

But Abraham
While holding the poor man
In his arms
Said they would not believe
Even if one came back
From the dead.

So
It is by faith

In The Word
That brings eternal joy
And peace
Beyond understanding.

*

The crystal crows are flying
From east to west
And the artist
Opens his inner eye
To the encompassing.

There is
A quiet to the air
As absence covers
The here and now.

Although
Time and space present
The close at hand
The artist yearns for the beyond
Where things speak
Of the treasure of life.

It is not
That life, in itself
Is meaningless
But that there is more
To being toward Truth
Than the surface.

Then
A quickness
Charges the moment
When ideation plunges
The mind
Into the vastness
Of what is there.

It is
This forevermore
That unites
The artist to the muse
As the crystal crows
Watch over the landscape.

How
The mind searches
Through hidden meaning
To grasp the unknown
As the muse
Dances
Into a portal to the beyond.

Then
The artist touches
The authentic article
And his offering
Becomes a still life
Of things in themselves.

Then
The crystal crows bring the living
To life.

*

In the darkness
The Spirt of Tuth
The Spirit of Truth
Offers a way
To the light
And the muse stirs
The mind
To see beyond thought
As the close at hand
No longer exists.

Symbols
Of another language
Arrange themselves
Into equations
Of form and substance
And the artist
Tastes
The wonders
Of the unknown.

It is
A message from the deep
That transcribes
Time and space

Into hope
As The Word
Anoints being toward Truth
With the authentic article.

Then
A light comes
From within
And visions
Of phenomenal reality
Dot with time past.

Through the earth
Of the always already there
The artist brushes
Truth into the moment.

Although
What is unknown
Pyramids being in time
Into a history
Of faith
The muse spirits
A dwelling place
Inside the mind.

How
Truth unburdens the mind
As The Unknown God
Witnesses the grieving
As being overthrows

Nothingness
And what no longer matters
Slips away
From the integrated collective.

So
The artist illustrates
The unknown with his blood.

How
Beautiful the language of Truth.

*

As the muse
Pulled the artist
Into deep trance
Being in nothingness
Appeared
In the other side
Of what was there.

Then
A vision surfaced
Of form and substance
A glorious image
Transcending language
And the artist
Opened his inner eye
As time left the scene
To a moment.

The grandeur
Of bring there
Before The Unknown God
Made him fall
To his knees
And he surrendered
All that he was.

When the moment
Was free of thought
The artist met
With The Spirit of Truth
And he wept
Before his epiphany.

He was far away
In a distant horizon
Where being in time
Intertwined
With hope and desire.

He wanted peace
A true mind and a pure heart
As the sight
Brought power
From the encompassing.

Then
His faith in The Word
Surfaced
And the muse took

Him back
Into the here and now.

The moment
Extended over
The close at hand
As his face
Looked into a looking glass
Where the integrated collective
Brought him a true mind.

So
The crystal crow gave his self
To a landscape
Where the artist heard a voice
That was his own
And the power
Of The Unknown God
Brought peace
For his pure heart.

*

A free spirit calls
To the artist
And it is the crystal crow
Pointing the way
To destiny.

With a brush
He paints connectivity
To the landscape
As wave upon wave
Of being toward Truth
Breathes life
Into the moment.

Asserting the Truth
He places
A hidden meaning
Into the calculus
Of mountains
And the curve
Of the moon.

Light and dark
Configure space
With the rise of mountains
And the fall of pitch.

It is
That darkness weighs more
Than light
And it settles in the frame
Of possibility
As the earth of being.

The other side
Of what is there
Shares the moment

As the muse ventures
Far, far away.

The artist paints
With a true mind
And a pure heart
As time
Reaches a stop.

So
The painting
And the landscape, itself
Are one
Joined by the blood
Of being toward Truth
As life pictures
The beginning and end
Of all and everything.

It is
A mountain scene
During apocalypse
Where destiny
Removes its mask.

*

It is
That the artist
Who looked
Beneath the given

Probed the close at hand
Finding a beauty
In the mystery
Of hidden meaning.

From the mountain ridges
He painted the dawn
Of everything
As mist rose
From the surroundings.

So
It was that being
Transcended time and space
As the artist
Saw the beginning
Before time
As governed
By the cosmic clock.

As vertical time
Defines
The always already there
The beginning becomes
More of a function
Of language
Than phenomenal reality.

There is
No beginning
To the cosmic clock

Because it is
The record of eternity
As being defines
The unknown.

So
The celestial clock
Governs the existence
Of the other
As things in themselves
And the physics
Of what is there
Lives in the mathematics
Of the concealed.

Linear time
Is the province
Of the biological clock
And the ground
Of being toward Truth
As days roll
From time past
To time present
And time future.

It is
Through faith
That the artist was given
The muse

As a guide to beauty.

*

As being toward Truth
Enters a particular portal
Images of eternity
Flourish
And the rhythm of drums
Keeps a steady heart.

There is
A light to the moment
That takes the artist
Behind time and space
Beyond the known
As the muse
Consumes absence.

It is
That being beyond self
Adheres
To the form and space
Of the ethereal
As the architecture
Of what is reveals
His essence.

With an anchor
In the here and now
The mind

Transcends the moment
As the muse
Forms images
Inside phenomenal reality.

Then
As the mind left
The body
The artist joined
To the flight of the crystal crow
As it pronounced
Time present
Into the always already there.

So
It is destiny
That brought him
To the everlasting
As the crystal crow chanted
In the wind.

Then
The artist rejoiced
With the embrace
Of the muse
And being in nothingness
Went their separate ways.

It is
A moment filled
With the authentic article

As being beyond self
Sees behind the mask
Of the other.

So
All the while
The biological clock
Of the artist
Is suspended.

*

As moves on
The artist touches
Outliving self
But the muse
Pulls him
Into the secret life
Of the always already there.

It is
His destiny
To paint meaning
Into the now
And he is thankful
For the calling.

Then
His inner eye awakens
And he sees
In the expanse

A tree on a hill.

At that moment
There is no other side
To being toward Truth
As the green of the tree
Overwhelms what is
And the muse
Pushes
The artist into the center
Of mind.

Then
A memory surfaces.

Her was tied down
Secured to a bed
When the sun rose
Tracing eternity
On the gold wall.

The sound
Of crows dwelt
With the living
As two old men
One black, one white
Walked to the tree
Together.

Then
They sat there

The shade
A refuge from the heat.

Time and space
Went away
As the tree burst
Into flames
And the two men
Rose
Into the sky.

So
In the living moment
Being in nothingness
Left a mark in the given.

*

When the mind
Fills with absence
And the heart pounds
Death into life
How time wears thin.

Then
The purpose of the artist
Turns dark
Because the muse
Cannot be found.

Outliving the self
Defines the moment
And the artist struggles.

As shades of darkness
Try to bury him
He remembers
The call to his heart
The call of Truth.

Then
Crows fly overhead
Their signal a refreshing turn.

Then
The roar of a train
Passes by
Out of the unknown.

Looking
Into the no longer
The artist pulls himself
Up out of the grave
As he searches
For hope.

In the hollow of mind
Time and space
Emanate a vision
As the self stirs
In the light of Truth.

It is
The battle between light
And darkness that he sees
As a portrait
In the looking glass.

His face is scared
And an ear is gone
But his voice
Carries a resolve
As he sees no Truth
In nothingness.

The artist
Does not surrender
To despair.

Now
He embraces the muse.

*

As the sky lit
With flames
The artist paints a man
With no shadow.

He stands tall
Bearded
And with pride
In his look

But he is alone.

Separating himself
From the other
He sees time and space
Pass him by
As the sky burns
A hold in mind.

Then
A hooded man
Walks forward carrying
A skull
Into the now
As images of spirits
Pyramid through the known.

How quiet the moment
As the substance
Of being
Ejects a silent scream
Into possibility
In measures of form
Covered with a mask
Of phenomenal reality.

There is no
Time to the moment
As the biological clock
Of the artist pauses
For a look into the abyss.

There is
The stumbling of thought
As nothingness
Portrays an image
Of self-deception
And the artist feels the depth
Of being alone
With himself.

So
The muse is no longer
And the artist
Carves
The brutality of a world
Inside the other.

Then
He thinks himself
Into a view of self
And the moment is gone.

*

In the garden
Far away
From time and space
The artist reaches
Through a portal
Into the substance
Of what matters.

There
He finds the image
Of the muse.

How
Possibility engulfs
The present
As the crystal crow calls out
To being toward Truth.

A stirring
Of phenomenal reality
Releases beauty
Into the moment
As the garden closes down
For autumn.

Although the muse
Is gone
The artist is touched
By the wilds
And he grows
Into the spirit
Of now.

Then
The mind latches onto
The moment
When the crystal crow occupies
the now
and being in nothingness

wage war
between Truth
and illusion.

There is no
Deception in beauty
But only the true light
Of forevermore.

There is only
The romance of being
And time
In the dance
Through a gauntlet
Where the living
Breathes life
Into form and substance.

As light fills
The garden with want
And need
The artist portrays
The longing for Truth
As angels trumpet
Into the heart
Of being toward Truth.

How
The wilds
Spoken by the crystal crow
Occupy

The always already there.

*

There is
A mystery to the sky
Unsolved
Through times and times
And a half.

There is
The unknown
Of the out there
And in the here
As the artist approached
The moment.

Opening
His inner eye
He saw images
Of another side
Following the rhythm
Of the heart
As drums rumble on.

The pulse
Of the universe
Clung
To the blood
Of being toward Truth
And life

Cried out
For understanding.

It was
An interlude of pity
And not punishment
That dressed the scene
And the crystal crow took
To the beyond.

From the celestial clocks
Eons fell
Into lost memories
As the origin
Of what mattered
Left a remnant
In traces of the mind.

So
In the face of possibility
The artist drew
The compass of being toward Truth
And the crystal crow
Counted the milestones
Of being in time.

How
The depths undressed
The concealed
Of phenomenal reality
As a song

Filled the artist's heart
With colors of the other.

Tension.

In that moment
The crystal crow summoned
The call of the wild.

*

In the close at hand
A mocking bird sings
As the wilds
Entertain in the garden.

While the crystal
Of the sky
Pronounces the presence
Of the beyond
The artist listens
To the groans
Of being toward Truth.

It is
Evident that the mind
Seeks transcendence
When dwelling
In nothingness
Since the authentic article
Is experiential

After the beyond.

The artist listens
To the drum of eternity
As mind
Leaves the body
And the illusion
Of the objective reality
Succumbs to oblivion.

Then
Insects think their way
Into what is
As silence visits
The angels.

So
From hope
Springs dreams
As the self
Launches into the unknown
And the artist searches
For a portal
To what matters.

Redefining being toward Truth
The artist hears
A blue jay
As time and space
Begin anew.

So
The biological clock
Of the artist
Holds the subjective
And the celestial clock
Governs the objective.

So
Being in the garden
Of now matters.

*

As being toward Truth proceeds
Through time and space
His biological clock
Unearths destiny
And the artist
Thinks his way
Through the looking glass.

It is
His seeing himself
As the other
That unravels
The mind
And that penetrates
The moment.

It is
A starlit night

That brings him close
To the root
Of his being
As silence opens
What is
To possibility.

Then
The artist enters
An interlude
When touching
The unknown
Becomes what is.

The artist, himself
Becomes a transfusion
Of what matters
And his look
Into the depth
Of the sky
Allows him to reach
Into the depths
Of being in time.

How
Silent the hidden meaning
That surrounds
The self
As nothingness
Assumes a presence.

Then
A portal appears
And the artist.
Enters it
To find The Spirit of Truth
As he believes himself
Into being toward Truth
As his biological clock
Approaches
A time of epiphany.

So
Each day has
A beginning and an ending
And the artist
Pictures the dominion
Of phenomenal reality
As hope.

*

Upon the integrated collective
Images appear
And the artist feels
His way to being toward Truth.

It is
A play of light
Through the shallows
Of time and space
That a picture forms

From the substance
Of the beyond.

Ever deeper into trance
He gathers a look
As his mind sketches
Being in nothingness.

It is
The calculus of life
Configured in a two-
Dimensional reality
That grows
Into forms of color
As the muse sings
Through the corridors
Of time.

Then
The muse builds
The face
Of what matters
As time past invades
Time present.

How
Lovely is the muse.

So
The dance
Of the moment

Infuses an idea where
Life begins
And the artist
Breathes the origin
Of being in time.

It is
An illumination
Of what matters
As she feeds him
With the energy
Of another kind.

All at once
The universe implodes
As the rush
Of being toward Truth captures
The end
Of all and everything
Except The Unknown God.

Then
Another universe begins.

*

There is
A presence
In time and space
Of a moment
Where the outer

And inner intersect.

As mind eclipses
The other
Being in time
Open
To a gauntlet
Leading to a place
Where thought begins.

Here
There is an energy
That emanates
The Spirit of Truth
And the artist reaches
Into the deep
To declare what is.

Then
An image appears
On the integrated collective
And a sad-eyed face
Looms
Across the horizon.

There is
A purity embedded
In the tears
Of the authentic article
Across the horizon.

There is
A purity embedded
In the tears
Of the authentic article
Speaking through
Outliving self
Yet
There is a dignity
In enduring.

To touch
The Spirit of Truth
As the mind transcends
Empirical reality
Brings
As moment
Of being toward Truth
In the presence
Of what matters.

How
The mind awakens
When immersed
In this epiphany
As the mined
Dwells in clarity
And images
Of The Spirit of Truth
Reconcile
A troubled heart.

So
Being toward Truth
Transcends the drift
Of meaning.

So
Being toward Truth rides
The waves of meaning.

*

Then
The artist turned
To the sound
Of the crystal crow
And time found
Its way to the moment
Of transcendence.

To seek
The origin of ideation
How The Spirit of Truth
Inhabits
A true mind and a pure heart.

As the unknown
Humbles the artist
He perceives
The coming and going
Of the concealed
As hidden meaning

Is struck
By the way. The truth
And the life.

So
The beyond
Invites the artist
To visit
The substance of being
As forms
Of what is
Declare things in themselves.

Images
Of another reality
Emanate
Through the trance
And the crystal crow
Signals a time
Of wonder.

The trance
Is not an escape
From the now
But the grounding
Of the totality
Of being.

Then
The muse lit a light
In the far reaches

Of presence
As the mind
Encompasses possibility.

So
The rhythm
Of the cosmic clock
Infuses the artist
With the breath
Of the authentic article
And being toward Truth
awakens
in the unknown.

Each day is
A visitation
With the unknown.

*

To know
As the river knows
As the crystal crow knows
How
The connection
Between being in time
Lifts a vision
Through a portal
And onto the integrated
Collective.

It is
A probing of the unknown
That displays the moment
As transcendent
And the artist seizes
What is there.

Then
In the passage
Of energy
The unreal affirms
Possibility
As he peels off
The mask of the real
Resulting
In a leap of faith.

So
The muse allows him
To look behind
The close at hand
To the always already there
The given
Of what matters.

It is
The workings
Of the inner eye
That penetrates the expanse
As the river
Feeds the moment

With the substance
Of the crystal crow.

So
Knowledge grows
Through the exercise
Of understanding
And the muse
Takes to the wind
Uncovering the concealed.

Time and space
Unfold
Into a vast region
Where the crystal crow stands
As a servant of Truth.

How meaning
Forms the cornerstone
Of knowledge.

*

In the shadows
Of being in time
Lurk the forces
Of hidden meaning
And the integrated collective
Shows them
Through a portal
In being toward Truth

185

The inner eye.

How
The mind searches
Through what is there
As if possibility
Did not exist.

So
The artist looks
Into the spirit
Of a thing
To uncover whole regions
Of the concealed.

Worlds come
And worlds go
As the mind sees
The close at hand
And reaches
For hidden meaning.

So
The disguise
Of hidden meaning
Is the concealed.

So
Behind the smile
Is a seething sea
Of tears

As the muse removes
The mask
Of being in nothingness.

Then
The celestial clocks
Point
To the beginning
Of what matters
As the heart
Feels its way
Through a gauntlet
Heading to Truth.

Knowledge, then
Extends
Into the possible
And the artist
Arranges his world
In magnitudes
Of being
And images of being.

There
Is the beginning
Of the future
As a now point
As a fiction.

So
It is a matter

Of being conscious
In the moment
For time present
Is an expanse
An interlude carried
By being toward Truth.

*

Looking
Upon the integrated collective
Into the reality
Beyond the shadows
On the cave wall
The artist captures
The now
As a moment
A duration of consciousness.

There
In the province of being
Stirs an image
Out of time and space
As the artist
Follows the muse
Into the deep.

Then
A ladder appears
And the artist
Climbs

Out of himself
As the mined
Listens
To the sounds
Of being toward Truth.

It is
Raining and a cathedral
Radiates with life.

So
The integrated collective
Connects the artist
To the image
Of what is there
While the muse
Moves his spirit
Into the encompassing.

Then
A room comes
Into the circle
Of what is there
And the artist
Portrays a presence
Within red walls.

A pool table
Fastens the light
Of the moment
Into the always already

There
As clouds of smoke
Temper the scene.

The game is over
And the players are gone.

It is
Late and the room
Fills the integrated collective
With a void.

SECTION 4:

shadows

Although the moon
Is there
And then gone
The mind reshapes
What is
As the now.

Absent
From being toward Truth
Thoughts run deep
Escaping the grip
Of the close at hand.

So
The artist bonds
With the moon
And a rip
Of melancholy
Tempers his spirit.

Times
And times and a half
Follow the moment
As self
Begins to belong
To the unknown.

There is
Distance between his
Thought
And the moon

As well as an absence
Of being who he is.

As the muse surrounds him
With the other
She feels his way
Into form and substance.

How
The other can fill
The moment
With phenomenal reality
As the artist touches
The quick point
Of the universe.

Then
The Spirit of Truth
Occupies
The time and space
Of the artist
As his eyes step out
Of a fog.

Then
The muse takes
His look
Into the now
As the grounding
Of his self establishes
A view

Of what matters.

How
Rich the earth
Of being toward Truth
As the moon fades
Into a new day.

So
There is life for now.

*

Surfacing
On the integrated collective
The crystal crow speaks being
And nothingness
Into the moment
As meaning hides
And Truth remains
Silent.

The bones ache with want.

The mind topples into darkness.

There are boots
Waiting for the signal
To attack
As the dawn retreats
Into the unknown.

The mission is
Simple:
To liberate meaning
And bring Truth
To the language
Of the here and now.

It is
In his painting
That the artist
Emanates a message
Beyond the sound of worlds
Infusing the gut
With a force
Powerful and lasting
While the mind
Embedded
In celestial dimensions
Looks on.

Seeded in the moment
The artifact
Assumes a mask
And the crystal crow
Interjects a portal.

The painting is
The portal
That transcends
Time and space
As being toward Truth ignites

A blast orbiting
About the other.

The signal is set.

The boots lock and load.

The moment of Truth approaches.

The crystal crow hungers.

*

So
The authentic article
Endows being toward Truth
With a truth
And the crystal crow signals
The coming of a portal.

It is
Over the last horizon
That the artist
Finds
The way to visions
Beyond phenomenal
Reality
And the mind
Takes flight with the crystal crow
Into forevermore.

In the gauntlet
Of being in time
The muse dispatches
Meaning
As the ground of Truth
And the artist
Absorbs the moment.

Then
The celestial clocks
Alter the course
For a truer destiny
One
When trumpets
Awaken the dead
To epiphany.

Then
A light from within
Reveals
The authentic article
In being toward Truth.

Truth stands still.

Meaning is silent.

Then
Knowledge fastens itself
To the moment
As the close at hand

Fills
With signals from beyond.

There is
A beauty in this time
That conquers
Outliving the self.

How
Hope awakens faith
In the way, the truth
And the life.

What a joy it is
To serve
The Unknown God.

*

With a pure heart
And a true mind
The artist pursues
Truth
As the muse leads
The way
Through the unknown.

Awakened
To the moment
When times and a half
Bleed with meaning

The artist plunges
Thought into visions
Of what matters.

Then
The Spirit of Truth
Takes him
Into the beyond
Where his essence
Leaves the body
And the mind
Of what is there
Liberates the present.

What power
Is infused
Through faith in The Word
And the artist seizes
Being in time
As nothingness disappears.

So
The moment launches
Dreams
Of a house
Of many mansions
The place
On the other side
Of time and space
And the artist
Takes the hold

Of the muse.

A chasm breaks loose
Between bring there
And the close at hand
As the muse
Prepares him
With the chimes
Of the cosmic clock.

Then.
The Unknown God
Blesses the faithful
And they give thanks.

*

In the valley
Of the forgotten
Spirits and ghosts
Stir in the fog
And being
Traverses that space
Following the flight
Of the crystal crow.

It is
A battlefield
Where the war
Of principalities
Rages in silence.

How
The heart opens
Possibility
As life begins
A new death.

So
The evil
Of the ghosts
Is outweighed
By the spirits of good
And the crystal crow
Navigates
Through the carnage
With the power
Of The Unknown God.

There is
A sign to the moment
That calls
Upon the mind
To attack nothingness
A place of no hope.

There is
But one way out
Of the interlude
And the crystal crow
Knows it well.

Then
Armed with the sword
Of righteousness
The muse joins in
The battles against
The demons
And the artist calculates
Being in time
In measures of faith
In The Word.

then
ten thousand thousand angels
gather around
The Spirit of Truth
In the valley
Of the living.

So
The artist paints
Victory
In the heart
Of being toward Truth.

*

So
The artist traveled
Across the expanse
Where time
Makes memories

Into a truth
And he turns
To the muse
For understanding.

He assumes he
Exists
And that he has
A life
But he knows
For sure
That that may not
Be true.

Then
He hopes his way
Through what is there
Following meaning
Looking through life
And he becomes
Being toward Truth.

Where being is
Ethereal
Being toward Truth is grounded
In the affirmation
Of self
And the going
Beyond self
Identifying the other.

If there is the other
It tells of a truth
That he is mirrored from.

Is he a reflection
Or a shadow
He does not know
For sure
But it seems as though
That being toward Truth
In a span of time
Leads him to believe
He exists.

So
The muse dwells
In the close at hand
And is grounded
In what matters.

She is his navigator
And he is the pilot
Of his being.

So
The artist thinks
His way
Into existence
As the processing

Of his memories.

*

The crystal crows are
In flight
Traversing the wisdom
Of time and space
As being toward Truth
Heads to the light
Of another beginning.

How
He suffered
In times past
With his wounds
Deep and debilitating.

How
He endured the torture
Of times and times
And a half
As the forces
Of evil
Beat him down.

In a large foyer
He stood
His feet bleeding
As the moment
Brought gods

Before him.

Crazed by torment
He saw them
And the architecture
Of their being
Yet
He did not trust
The moment
As he turned to his faith
In The Unknown God.

Writhing in pain
He crawled
Alongside the living
As he tasted
His own blood
From wounds
Ever so deep.

Then
An image of a man
Wearing darkness
Projected into times
And evil
Spilled throughout
The room.

It was
That this agony
Was pushed upon him

To alter his faith
But he did not waver.

In his confusion
He turned to The Word
And was not denied.

From this interlude
He came to know
That there is
No hope, no faith
In hell.

*

Here
Upon the edge
Of oblivion
Where the mind
Ventures
The artist views
The eclipse
Of being toward Truth.

Nothingness fills
The expanse
And the crystal crow pulls
In an horizon of hope.

Staggered
By the enormity

Of the wilderness
The artist
Portrays mountains
As the imprint
Of what matters.

There is
No time to the moment
Although the self
Feels the heart beat
Of the wilds.

Then
The other makes
An overture
And nothingness
Goes away.

So
Their bond
In the moment
Births meaning
And the crystal crow
Dances through the air.

It is being to being
That brings an indwelling
Of substance
In what is there
As the artist enters
The mountain

Of what matters.

The mountain
The crystal crow
And the other
Climb into being toward Truth
As the picture
Of all
That is there
Acquires power and strength.

Then
Form follows substance
Into an image
Of wonder.

*

Through a portal
In phenomenal reality
The inner eye
Scanned the unknown
A wilderness of things
As absolutes.

It was
An alien world
Where the mind
Braved
As images of truths
Were frightening

But there was
A window
Between the artist
And what was there.

Then
He reached deep
Into his substance
And saw
Layers of absolutes
And as he passed
From one layer
To another
The view became horrific.

Turning
To the network
Of his mind
He read the glyphs
Of time and space
Present
As images approaching
The vile and dark.

So
The outside eclipsed
The inside
And a gauntlet
Of compounded terror
Led to another side.

Then
The crystal crow lifted him
From what was there
Bringing him
To a river valley
Of calm.

When his trembling stopped
He saw a passage
Of grace and peace
And there he laid
His body down.

Being toward Truth
Found comfort
In that absolute.

*

Beyond the close at hand
Truth breathes in
What matters
As phenomenal reality
Feeds the moment.

There is
A light to the time
When the mind
Collects meaning
As it drifts
Across the integrated

Collective.

It is
The cosmic consciousness
That transcends
Being toward Truth
As the artist moves
deep
wit1hin trance
and her touches
Truth.

Then
Substance takes
The form of the crystal crow
And self
Assumes being toward Truth.

It is
In the wilds of being
That Truth surfaces
As time and space
Drop away.

Truth
As the absolute
Pictures a reality
That appears
As the ground
Of what is there
And the artist goes

Beyond being
And nothingness
To the moment
Of now.

There lives Truth.

There is the alpha
And omega
Of all and everything.

There
Is the portrait
Of being toward Truth
As the crystal crow signals
The self
With the redemption
Of time.

So
There is the Way
The Truth and the Life
As absolute.

*

As the confusion
Between being in nothingness
Buried the artist
He experienced
The depth of evil

And the height of good.

His life
Was taken to extremes
And then his muse
Took him
To an even place.

In his delirium
He experienced
The visions that made him
An artist.

So
He suffered
But it came about
That the pain
He went through
Brought him insights
That transcended
Being in time.

It became
His purpose
To depict beauty
And the wonder
Of being toward Truth.

Remembering his angst
He drove himself
Beyond it

With the help
Of the muse.

Then
He drank in the power
Of The Unknown God
Seeing the substance
Of what mattered
And his artifacts
Exploded
With meaning.

It was
That he experienced
The magnitude
Of nothingness
And how it
Destroyed hope
But he endured
Finding his mission.

What joy to capture
The awesome symmetry
Of what is there.

*

A chill crossed
Against him
As the grey sky
Fostered no hope

For sunshine.

The leaves gathered
Around his feet
As he looked to the trees
On the mountain ridges.

How time
In the living present
Spoke to his bones
And the artist
Focused
On one barren tree.

It spoke of life
And death
As well as the eternal
And the crystal crow targeted
The unknown.

Two vultures circled
Up high
And then lit
On the tree
As the rumble
Of a train
Awoke the moment.

The artist drew
On times and times
And a half

When death visited
His thoughts
And he viewed
The tree
As a symbol
Of carrying on.

He was a type
Of survivor equipped
With a razor's edge
His mind keen
And sharp.

How
The chill
Of that day
Infused The Spirit of Truth
Deep
Within being toward Truth.

How
An awakening
Showed him
The depth of the unknown.

Then
The vultures were gone
As the crystal crow
Articulated being

And nothingness.

*

Toward being toward Truth
The cosmic consciousness
Whirled with images
As time and space
Traced what mattered.

It was
A time when the crystal crow
A free spirit
Registered thoughts
Of Truth
And that which is
Absolute.

The artist
Lifted his view
Revealing
The interstices of mind
And the muse
Provided a window
Into the unknown.

Approaching a light
The artist held
To the chasm
Between being
And nothingness

As his biological clock
Touched the rhythm
Of the given.

How
Waves of eternity
Eclipsed thoughts
As the crystal crow
Brought sustenance
To a moment of hunger.

So
The artist tapped
Into the cosmic
Consciousness
And the mind pictured
Love
As an absolute.

There was
Faith, hope and love
But the greatest
Of these was love.

Then
Time and space
Opened
To visions thought
Impossible
As the muse warped
Time

And a portal edged
Into what was there.

It was
A portal to the other.

*

How
The mind searches
For meaning
As Truth hides
Within the close at hand.

It is
An archeology of thought
And the artist digs
Beneath what is there
To get at the rubric
Of being in time.

He finds
Among the living
The breath of hope
Yet
Eyes are closed
To what matters.

To open
The landscape to view
The artist touches

The unknown
Uncovering the concealed.

Then
The inner eye sees
The other
And it grows
Within mind.

To be
At the edge of darkness
A place impenetrable
By light
The artist builds
A kingdom
Out of colors
As the cosmic consciousness
Spreads
From horizon to horizon.

So
Thoughts link one
To another as dominoes
And an absolute rises
From their fall.

It is Truth
Forming in the heart
Of being toward Truth.

*

How
Driven the artist
To capture the battle
Between being
And nothingness
As his biological clock
Tunes
Into a parabola of time.

Seeing all sides
As a single plane
Allows him to probe
The unknown.

It is
An entry into the cosmic
Consciousness
That he has achieved
As time and space
Yield their secrets.

So
The engine
Of being toward Truth drives
The artist
Into possibility
As he gathers
The authentic article.

Kneeling
In a graveyard

Where thoughts perish
The artist presents
The presence of life
And the shadows
Of life.

It is
The architecture
Of the beyond
As mind configures
The symmetry
Of immortality.

Then
Being in time awaken
The moment
To the rhythm of the given.

So
There is the mystery
Of mind.

*

In the garden
Of tables and chairs
Angels dance
To the rhythm
Of the cosmic clock.

Alleluias fill the air.

In the substance
Of his being
The artist sees
Time and space
As an adventure
Into the beyond
As he notes
The cosmic consciousness.

Beauty is first
Defined in terms
Of The Unknown God
And the majesty
Of The Word.

So
There is the birth
Of beauty
As the wonder
Of The Spirit of Truth
Shapes
What matters.

Touching the substance
Of that wonder
The artist
Reaches being toward Truth
As an entrance
Into things in themselves.

Then
The crystal crow carries Truth
Across being in time
And the artist
Finds the mind
Of the absolute.

So
Time and space
Convey being toward Truth
Into an epiphany
As beauty embraces
The moment.

*

As the inner eye
Enters
The cosmic consciousness
And being toward Truth rises
Out of the body
The artist envisions
Things in themselves.

Visiting in the past
With those
Who knew better
He frames
Time and space
With a man
With one ear.

To see
Into deep space
Where the mind
Searches
For beauty
He finds the breath
Of life
And trials in life.

From surviving
The combat
Between being
And nothingness
He emerges
Into the breath
Of what matters
And he sketches
The brutality
Of what is there.

How
The heart pounds
For mercy
And the painting
Does not lie.

So
True beauty grows
From suffering
As a compass
Leaves no trace

Of relief.

Then
The crystal crow lights
On a lamp post
Offering kinship
To the end.

*

Climbing out
Of the person he was
The artist tasted
The breath of the other
And the wheels
Of the celestial clock
Took a turn
Into eternity.

Howe
The mind projects
Being toward Truth
As time past dissolves
In a looking glass
And the reflection
Of what matters
Fills times
And times and a half
With wonder.

Then
Thoughts abstract
The universe
And linear time
Leaps
Into nothingness.

In this moment
Being toward Truth connects
With the absolute
And Truth shines
From the cosmic
Consciousness.

So
The mind takes
What is there
Positioning the dominos
In an array
That allows the artist
To flourish
With the authentic article.

How
Radiant the moment
When the mind
Finds within the unknown
The energy
Of possibility.

It is
Through the other
That the artist
Seizes
A portal to immortality.

So
Possibility
Is the energy
That drives the mind.

*

A slow rain
Greets the morning
With a green tree
Turned to gold
And the artist
Mirrors its image
In silent repose.

There is
A dignity to its form
The dignity
Of beauty
Caught in an autumn
Rain.

He touches
The thing in itself
And releases

Its life
To the wilds.

There is
A particular freedom
In being toward Truth
As he
Lifts the concealed
From the unknown
As the tree suspends
The invisible
In the quick of its beauty.

How
The wonder of life
Moves the substance
Of being into places
Where thoughts are born
And the artist
Takes what is there
Into the flight
Of the crystal crow
Across all horizons.

So
It is the calculus
Of the unknown
That triggers beauty
To dance
Before all eternity.

So
Beauty dwells
In the eternal
Within the close at hand
Revealing the design
Of being toward Truth.

*

Following the flight
Of crows
The artist measures life
Into the beyond
And the muse reads
The destiny
Of existence in shadows
Of being toward Truth.

To be
In the frontier
Of being
The mind shapes
What is there
As the artist
Travels through a portal
To the given.

As linear time
Falls away
The celestial clocks
Present the reality

Of what is here
In the unknown.

In a moment
Time present expands
Across possibility
And the crystal crow
Launches a look
Into the cosmic
Consciousness.

Truth
In its many forms
Points
To the absolute
That is beyond
Understanding
Yet
Is believed
To be there.

So
In the universe of being
There are many truths
And each traces
Its origin
Through the authentic article
To The Unknown God.

Here
There is no deception

As life expands
Into the other
And the spirit
Of the crystal crow
Inspires the artist
To picture the anatomy
Of Truth.

*

As the artist
Crawls into the cosmic
Consciousness
Secrets emerge.

They are shadows
Of the here and now
And silent treasures.

Six vultures drift by
Their eyes seeking
A harvest of death
And the mind
Calculates
The flight of life.

From the expanse
The artist shapes
Being in time
Ads the colors of eternity
Reveal Truth.

On his canvas
He portrays a portal
That leads
Outside of time and space.

It is
On the other side
Of death
Where the muse
Undresses being toward Truth.

Naked before the absolute
The artist pulls
His mind
Out of darkness
As the vultures circle.

Then
Possibility opens
To the wind
And time
Is blown away.

So
It is the rule
Of the cosmic clock
That determines
The authentic article.

*

It is
That angels define
This moment
When being toward Truth
Emerges
Onto time and space
And a simple truth
Suggests reaching
The absolute.

As part
Of the cosmic
Consciousness
The artist infuses
Possibility
Where nothingness
Claimed dominion.

Then
The moment fills
With song
As the anthem
Of eternity
Marches
Onto the close
At hand.

The angels display
Times and a half
As the here and now
And the artist forms

Beauty forevermore.

How
A truth leads
To the promise
That hopes and dreams
Will be fulfilled
And the artist
Calls upon the muse
To configure
What matters.

So
The lines
Of mortality circle
Being toward Truth
As the angels occupy
The mind.

So
Here and now
Become a leap
Onto forevermore.

*

Off in the distance
A beacon shows the way
To the authentic article
And time turns
To a moment

That is larger than itself.

There
Among waves
Of darkness
The artist draws
Upon mind
To measure the distance
To eternity.

It is
A grain of sand away
Yet
The artist sets
Being toward Truth
Within the cosmic
Consciousness.

Calling upon the muse
The artist finds
Deliverance
With The Spirit of Truth
And the house
Of many mansions
Opens its doors.

There
Among the radiance
Of The Word
The artist kneels
As an aria

Unfolds
Absolute majesty.

It is
A visitation
To a moment
That gives hope.

How certain
The artist is
That one day he will
Be
With The Unknown God
Forevermore.

*

It is
The love
For The Spirit of Truth
That opens the heart
To eternity
As the crystal crow confesses
The shadows
Of being toward Truth.

Autumn sets
The forest ablaze
In reds and golds
And the air
Is punctuated

With a chill.

So
Timer is
Always already there
As the peace
Beyond understanding
Fills the breath
With the authentic
Article.

As the artist feels
His way
Into the cosmic
Consciousness
The crystal crow sets the stage
For accessing
The other
And The Spirit of Truth
Saturates the expanse.

To be there
On the front line
Of being in nothingness
Builds muscle
Into hopes and dreams
And the artist
Listens to the story
Of the rainbow crow
As the lore of Natives
Brings sight to the blind.

How
Precious this existence
That brings life
To old bones.

*

Cutting through the silence
A siren whines
And tragedy strikes
With the edge of death.

The crystal crow sets course
Across the blue
And mind
Slips into trance.

Behind the gold
Of the trees
Traffic evidences
The trace of destination
As the artist pictures
The blue eyes
Of the muse.

She is his destination.

How
True is eternity
As the close at hand
Defines being toward Truth.

Then
The moment sketches
The absolute
As the muse dances
Across the sky
With the crystal crow
And a portal opens
The impossible.

As the wind
Causes the leaves
To applaud
The artist births
His colors into Truth
And his life turns
To a mocking bird
A treasure
Of being in time.

So
Autumn lives
In the heart
Of what matters
And the artist
Caresses the muse
And her thoughts.

*

Traveling
In a two-dimensional

Reality
The artist rides
A parabola of time
And eternity unfolds
In beauty and wonder.

Governed by celestial clocks
He speeds
Through a portal
Into things in themselves.

There
The muse reveals
Nothingness
And the crystal crow answers
The call
To being in time.

The mysteries
Of mind color what matters
As possibility has
No end.

Then
He greets the other
As a kindred spirit
And angels rejoice.

Riveted to the moment
The artist goes
Beyond

The close at hand
To the substance
Of what is there.

Then
The other births
Forevermore
As a wilderness
Of treasures
And a church bell
Chimes Truth
Into the moment.

So
It is written deep
Within mind
That meaning has
Purpose
As the artist moves
Time and space.

*

Into the other side
Of time and space
The mind
Leaves the body
In suspension
As the cosmic conscious
Brings being toward Truth
Through a portal.

There
The biological clock
Melts
And the artist
Races into the wilds.

The crystal crow
Marks the wilderness
With a call
From somewhere
And mind
Issues the inner eye
To see what matters.

The mystery
Of the authentic article
Stands in an opening
Where form
Consumes substance
And nothingness remains.

Then
The artist raises
His vision
To the celestial clocks
And he reaches
A milestone
To gather what matters.

So
There are three:

Beauty, Truth
And the absolute
As the artist proves
Their being
With a stroke
Of a brush.

To pursue these three
Is to touch eternity
With a pure heart
And a true mind.

*

As mind thinks
Its way
Through possibility
The close at hand
Traces what is there
And the artist pulls
From who he is
In view of nothingness.

How the heart
Reaches out
To the eternal
While death leaves
The artist in want.

As the muse
Entertains in the moment

With notions
Of the immortal
An old man
Stumbles
Through a looking glass.

While time and space
Collapse
The artist picks his way
With the painting
Of times and a half
And the muse
Brings a smile
To his face.

Then
A church bell
Tells of the hour
As one day follows
The next
And the muse
Gives the artist
A destiny.

So
The old man
Lives in the present
And is gone
Sooner or later
But for now
He gives thanks

For what he is.

*

As Truth
Emanates from the absolute
And time uncovers
The concealed
Things in themselves
Surface
And being toward Truth
Connects
To the cosmic conscious.

It is there
That the beginning
Of the authentic article
Bleeds into mind
And the artist
Projects the life
Of an old man.

As his biological clock
Turns toward
A milestone
The old man
Recedes
Into the close at hand
And the artist
Undresses
Times and a half.

To generate
His likeness
The muse looks
To the heavens
Draining the light
From stars
For the depth
In his eyes.

He is at
The edge of his self
As the artist
Portrays him
In a grave yard
Waiting for his tombstone.

He had never
Pictured himself
As an old man
For he thought
In his heart that he was
Forever young.

*

Traces
Of the other flash
Across the terrain
As the mind
Awakens in darkness.

There is
Doom written
Across the look
Of the other
Facing the mirror
Of Truth.

What promise
Is given
To one in darkness
And the artist
Paints the other
As a seafarer
With full beard.

He thinks himself
The captain
Of his destiny
While the celestial clocks
Spell
What is there.

To be the victim
Of his own thoughts
How folly
Vanquishes the self.

Then
He walks out
Of the darkness
Leaving doom behind.

He has seen
The light
Of amazing grace
And it gives him
The strength
To overcome.

So
All are victims
Of their indiscretions
And the captain turns
To the child within.

How
The beliefs of a child
Comfort the aged
With faith.

*

The crystal crows are
Coming
From the other side
Of what is there
And the artist
Plunges
Deep into trance
As his inner eye
Searches for Truth.

Time and space
Eclipse possibility
As he contends
With the absence
Of the here and now.

There is
A song in the air
As being toward Truth
Summons
Truth from the beyond.

Then
He wears
The authentic article
As the muse
Infuses him with images
Of being in time.

How
Treasures of wonder
Display a vigor
And his life
Becomes invisible
Married
To the cosmic conscious.

How
Times and a half
Leaves traces
In the blood

Of what matters
And the muse
Nourishes the moment
With visions.

As the crystal crow
Sets time and space
Into stillness and silence
The artist claims
The gift
Of blessed assurance.

*

With a face
Full of agony
A scream lets loose
Across ages
And the muse feels
The end
Of what matters.

One
Who knows the trauma
Of enduring pain
Lives long enough
To suffer more.

In the heart
Are vultures
Tearing at the flesh

Of life
And the artist
Knows the look.

Only
A broken mind
Tells this Truth
But the figure
Is not alone.

Humanity witnesses
This tragedy
As it weeps
With compassion.

How
A suffering child
Draws life
As terror rips
Through the moment.

It is
A child in Vietnam
Naked in her pain.

It is
A painting of fright
And the artist
Shares the tumult

Of war.

*

To go
Beyond what is there
To leave
The here and now
How the mind
Infused with possibility
Searches for Truth.

It is
The substance of mind
That the length
And breadth
Of being toward Truth
Comes true.

How
Beautiful the mountains
As the morning mist
Drifts in the hollows
And the artist
Seizes
The wonder
Of being toward Truth.

There are
Spirits in the wilderness
That occupy

Being in time
As the distance
Between here and there
Is a dream away.

As nothingness falls
From the sky
And the mind
Registers the moment
The muse embraces
The artist with fervor.

Then
Times and a half
Trace
The authentic article
Into the heart
And a thing in itself
Forms Truth.

So
Between here and now
And there and then
Is only a dream
As the mask of mortality
Hides the Truth
In the now.

*

It was
One of those days
When the sun beamed
Through the clouds
As shadows
Formed a patchwork
On the mountain ridges.

The leaves had fallen
And a chill
Coursed through the air.

An old man sat
In the garden
Of tables and chairs
Surrounded by sparrows
And he fed them
Bread crumbs.

He wanted
To teach them how
To sing
But they would not listen
As their chatter
Seemed without meaning.

Then
A goshawk flew down
And threatened them
And the old man
Watched

Startled by the sight.

Then
The goshawk was gone
And the sparrows
Hid
In the bushes.

The artist
Painted the scene
As if it mattered.

There was something
In the wind
That he did not
Understand.

So
Every day is
The last day.

*

At the beginning
Of nothingness
The artist saw
The abyss
As formidable
A space beyond time
Where being
Held no promise.

It was there
That he saw death
As his life
Filled with breath
And he turned
To a light
In the darkness.

At the very edge
Of oblivion
He sought meaning
And he opened
His eyes
To what was there.

The artist must continue.

It was
His duty and his destiny.

Pulling himself together
The artist reviewed
What he saw
And he knew the light
As the beacon of Truth.

He headed toward it.

It was
A number
Of milestones later

That he looked back
To nothingness
And it was still there.

Then
He passed a horizon
And heard
The sound of life.

It was
That nothingness
Was his to choose
Giving up
On life.

Truth was calling.

The artist must continue.

*

In the sky
A pure crystal blue
The sun warmed
The artist
As he conspired
To depict
Life as it was.

The crystal crows and the muse
Were in on it

But altered his view.

Then
The mind captured
A sight to remember.

It was
A portal near the edge
Of reason
And the artist
Leaped into it.

Spiraling
Through a tunnel
He throttled
All the more
And time and space
Disappeared
Into a heavy darkness.

Then
He saw a dog
With head bowed
At the side
Of an empty crib.

The infant was dead.

With bold strokes
He painted the loss
As being toward Truth

Pulled strings of remorse.

Outside a window
Crows landed
And the authentic article
Took to like.

In a corner
Of the universe
There was only weeping
And the crystal crows
Gathered
In being in nothingness.

*

As a train headed
North
The crystal crows went south
And a parabola of time
Lit the scene
With the artist
Posed
In the garden
Of tables and chairs.

He saw
The beginning of Truth
Wander by
As traces of the authentic
Article emanated

261

From a two-dimensional
Reality.

He noted
A number of crows
Pestering a hawk
And time and space
Emptied
Into the drift
Of things in themselves.

How
Freedom seems possible
As the heart pounds
Life
Into the moment.

Then
The artist saw
Flames
Engulf the continents
As time had
Run out.

How
Tragedy follows folly
As the proud annihilate
What is there.

Then
The hawk disappeared.

*

The mystery
Behind what is there
Ties knots
In the mind
As the artist seeks
The muse
To help him
With his vision.

There is
An opening in the sky
And light pours
Into the heart
Of being toward Truth.

The crystal crows are
About
And the artist
Speaks to them
As angels
Carry the moment
Into wonder.

Barren
The trees sleep.

Then
The artist climbs
Out of himself
To view a thing
In itself.

ombarded
By possibility
He closes his eyes
And mountains
Stretch into the beyond.

How
The inner eye
Sees
Past the here and now
And into what matters.

How
Eternity rises
Into view
And the muse
Infuses him
With the authentic article.

Then
The given brings
The artist
Into the company

Of The Unknown God.

*

Laughter
Over morning coffee
What a gift
As the garden
Of tables and chairs
Is lit
With good cheer.

How
The warmth
Of good friends
Touches the heart
With the passion
Of the living.

To be
Fully alive
What treasure
It is
And the artist
Depicts the grace
Of the dance
Between friends.

The talk of the crystal crowd
Bubbles
Being into the here

And now
With good spirits
And the muse
Delights the artist
With her sparkling eyes.

As fun
Teases the heart
The thought
Of the world
Is absent
And only the moment
Matters.

There is
No time to being toward Truth.

There is
Nowhere else
That exists.

How
The grace
Of The Unknown God
Offers all of this
As a blessing.

Thanks.

*

As linear4 time
Set the biological clock
The artist grew old
And images
Of magnitude dotted
Space.

It was
A leap into a parabola
Of time that brought
A two-dimensional reality
Through meditating
On The Word.

He found
That the splendor
In being toward Truth
Was nourished
By The Spirit of Truth
And that was
A Truth he cherished.

The secrets
Behind what was there
Wrote upon his mind
And the artist
Believed in them
As a message
From The Unknown God.

How
He stood strong
Before nothingness
As his life
Receded into oblivion
Yet
He thought himself
Into being true
To his self and beliefs.

A hawk sat
On a lamp post
As the crystal crow
Penetrated the quiet
With its piercing cry.

Then
The canvas took
The form of life
That meant more
As the artist
Entered
A vertical column
Of time.

*

In the center
Of the absolute
Thrives
The vertical column of time

As the close at hand
Becomes the shadow
Of being toward Truth.

It is
Perceived
Through the inner eye
And into the authentic
Article
The very element
Of the absolute.

So
The artist
And his muse
Connect
Alpha to omega
To create
A parabola of time.

From there
They collect
Visions of the eternal
While nothingness
Rips open their lives.

They
No longer are blind
To what matters
But dwell
In the wonder

Of Truth.

Their blood
Then comes
From a pure heart
Knowing the face
Of nothingness.

How
Their true mind
Colors the view
With the absolute
As being toward Truth
Leaves the ground
Of outliving the self.

*

A long day, a long week
Time wears thin
A mind in motion.

Deep
In the heart
Of being toward Truth
The self looks
For light
But finds darkness
And shadows
Of darkness.

So
The artist seeks
Truth
And the archeology
Of Truth
And he sifts
Through the dust
Of time
Hoping to find
Remnants
Of what matters.

Then
A c row lands
On a lamp post
And the artist
Engages his persona.

While wisdom hides
In the concealed
The muse unearths
What is there
And the crystal crow traces
Origins
Of being in nothingness.

To know
The ground
Of the past
Illuminates the cause
Of the close at hand

As the now
Bleeds
Into time and space.

Then
Faith in The Unknown God
Enlightens the artist
And he becomes one
With the authentic article.

*

To live
With the authentic article
While in the now
How the thought
Of death
Awakens being toward Truth.

Evert closer to the end
An old man
Measures his steps
Ass his balance
Leaves the given.

It is
In a cemetery
That he finds life
And he notices
The crystal crow perched
On a tombstone.

Time shifts
From alpha to omega
And the artist
Plays with grades
Of blue.

The old man
While sitting on a bench
Shakes hands
With destiny
As his name
Remains anonymous.

How
Figures drift
Across the landscape
As the mind
Struggles
With what matters.

There are
Times and there are times
And a half
While moments touch
Memories
And the artist paints
Truth
Based upon the always
Already there.

So
The old man lives
And that is enough
For him.

So
The artist paints
And that is enough
For him.

*

It is
Bb being toward Truth
Within the domain
Of the always already there
That the close at hand
Hides Truth
And the artist
Meditates
Upon what matters.

While he is
Deep into trance
The muse opens
His mind
To cosmic consciousness
And the sun
Approaches the end
Of his time.

So
His biological clock
Winds down
And the artist finds
A way to move
Into things
In themselves.

How
The celestial clocks
Furnishes choices
And the artist
Takes
To The Unknown God
For council.

Then
The sun disappears
And the moon turns to blood.

Then
The muse infuses
Visions
Into mind
And the artist touches
Truth.

Then
The crystal crow brings him
Bread
And his hunger

Goes away.

Then
His life warms
And he passes
Into the unknown
In search
Of peace beyond
Understanding.

*

So
The leaves dance
In the wind
And the mind drifts
Across mountains
How
The here and now
Play with being toward Truth.

To be
Caught up
In the moment
How
The self forgets
Itself
As it tumbles
Through the unknown.

Then
A rush of energy
Infuses the artist
With the will
To continue
Even though
Nothingness abounds.

How
Tragic is choice
Set by the celestial clocks
As the artist seeks
The substance
Of what is there.

Although
A broken man
He configures Truth
In a blaze
On a canvas
That tells times
A measure of wonder.

There is
A rumbling
In his heart
That brings him
To the here and now
Forevermore.

So
Truth anoints his vision
As his pain
Carries him
Into cosmic consciousness.

*

It is
That the mind
Is a mystery
And being
Is grounded
In assumption.

It is
As if what matters
Differs from one
To another
And reality is
A best guess.

So
There are no
Absolutes
And Truth is
Shades of gray.

Then
The artist opens
His inner eye

And the muse
Adds focus
To being toward Truth.

How
This moment
Imprints a meaning
That connects
The loose ends
Dangling
In the here and now
As The Word defines
All things
And the artist
Chooses a way
From alpha to omega
And back.

It is
In the image
Extracted
From what is there
That the artist
Speaks
And the language
Of being in nothingness
Is his chalice
Of the always already
There.

Drinking deeply
He orchestrates the music
Of the unknown.

*

With only
The inner eye
Open
The artist grasps
What is within
The substance
Of the given
And the muse sheds
Illusions
Of the here and now.

Meditating
Upon The Word
He finds a way
To what matters
Portraying it
In an image
Of the other.

Then
The crystal crow turns reality
Into a given
As the muse soars above.

To fixate
Upon what is
The artist passes
Into cosmic consciousness
And the always
Already there
Reveals the beginning
Of the absolute.

Extracting
An image out
Of a vision
The artist ignites
An eternal wonder
And the muse
Dives
Into mind.

There
Are the figures
Of being toward Truth
As a parabola of time
Links alpha to omega
As Truth surfaces
In the here and now
Of the crystal crow, a free spirit.

SECTION 5:

touching the other

To see the meat
Of being in nothingness
The artist connects
To cosmic consciousness
Leaving his self
To the given.

Approaching the end points
Of time and space
He captures
What is there
The essence
Of phenomenal reality.

Then
His mind follows
The image
Of the crystal crow
Across a landscape
Of fire.

Then
The muse brings
The rain
And it covers
All and everything.

Then
Time disconnects
The moment
And the artist

Follows the crystal crow
Through a portal
In the beyond.

As a vision stirs
The muse unmasks
Being toward Truth
And the artist
Drinks in
The authentic article.

He is
On the road
With paints, brushes
And canvas.

He is
Walking through time
And space
Walking
Through a parabola
Of time
And onto
What matters.

So
He becomes
The architect
Of his being.

*

In the half-light
Of a candle
The artist looks
To the muse
And she is there.

Being in time
Hold secrets
And cosmic consciousness
Constructs
A dwelling for them.

As the artist
Detaches himself
From the here and now
The muse carries
The candle
To the other side
Of a looking glass.

Then
The universe explodes
With thoughts
As the bells
Of eternity ring true.

There is
An indescribable love
That the muse has
For the artist
And a dynamic

Devotion the artist has
For the muse.

Together
They travel through time and space
Riding the substance
Id being toward Truth.

They define each other
With the authentic article.

Then
Others stand
With the forest
Of wonder
And the artist shares
The blood
Of a thing in itself.

How
Precious the treasure
Of humanity.

*

Truth
As a flame
In the darkness
How
Being toward Truth summons
What matters.

So
The artist displays
The authentic article
In a two-
Dimensional reality
And eternity
Fills the moment
With the always
Already there.

Tearing himself
From assumption
He activates
The transfer of mind
Into cosmic consciousness
And Truth
Becomes the close
At hand.

There are
Slices of the moment
Where Truth
Shines
As portals
Into the unknown
And being toward Truth
Rides
On a parabola of time
Beyond the here and now.

Then
The muse pulls
A dynamic wonder
That breathes in
The elements
Of the celestial clocks.

Then
The artist walks
Into destiny
With the hope
Of maintaining his dignity
And covering his miss steps.

How
The Spirit of Truth
Reviews the artist
With mercy
Because he keeps
The faith.

*

So
The wind carries
The flame of life
Into the heart
Of being toward Truth
And the muse
Connects the artist
To the other.

It is not
Merely the placement
Of color here
And dabs of color there
But it is
An epiphany
Of what is.

So
The muse sings
Truth
Into the moment
As time and space
Unchain
The beyond.

Then
Freedom
Launches a vision
Where Truth speaks
And the other
Touches
A moment awesome
In its power.

To liberate
The self
The artist seizes
The essence
Of what matters
And the muse

Moves his vision
Into the unknown.

Then
The celestial clocks
Open travel
Beyond the universe
And a journey
Of mind celebrates
The moment.

How
The image elevates
Being toward Truth.

*

Then
It was winter
And the artist envisioned
A place where life
Warmed death
And a star
Of the celestial clocks
Pointed to the birth
Of what matters.

How
What is there
Hides Truth
As the crystal crow answers

291

The call
Of the authentic article.

The trees
Barren to the bone
Sleep with dreams
Of another time
And the muse
Rubs thoughts
Into mind.

So
Which is primal:
Knowledge or faith.

It is
That knowledge hungers
For more
Where faith is sufficient
In itself.

It is
That the artist
Transcended the dull round
And all the reasons
For being toward Truth
Become secondary
To The Spirit of Truth.

To be
Is to serve

And the artist
Served
The Unknown God.

So
It was the fullness
Of time
That surpassed
The impossible
And an infant took
His first breath.

Then
The crystal crow entered
Eternity.

*

Ever deeper into trance
The artist follows
The muse
Into the unknown
Through a portal
Opening mind
To cosmic consciousness.

There are
Times
And times and a half
When moments
With the muse

Allow visions
Of possibility.

Then
What is
Is no longer
As the masks
Of the other
Drop away.

In the shadows
Of being toward Truth
The muse
Uncovers mystery
After mystery
And she shares
What IS there
As visions
That the artist grasps.

What is there
Becomes
The close at hand
With no hidden meaning
And the mountains
Awaken
With epiphany.

So
The muse takes
The artist

Through time and space
Until the image
Of being in nothingness
Defines the moment.

How
The artist adores
The muse
As life breathes life
Into being toward Truth.

*

So
All beauty is
A reflection
Of cosmic consciousness.

It is
The song
Of what matters
And a lure
Into the unknown.

To get
Out of self
And witness the secrets
Held by hidden meaning
How
The artist lives
Through being toward Truth

With the muse
Ever close.

She is the access to wonder.

Then
In the midpoint
Of all and everything
The muse allows
The artist to approach
Truth
As he rides
On the energy
Of the always already
There.

How
The moment emanates
Through the artist
As he meditates
Upon The Word
And he moves
Carefully
Through being
and nothingness.

So
All and everything
Is an element
In the formula
To perceive

Beauty as it is.

For the artist
The muse is true beauty
And pure wonder.

*

To hear the voice
Of the muse
How the artist thrives
In his moment.

Truth is
In the sound
Of her being
As she rubs meaning
Into his blood
Defining the presence
Of an absolute.

It is
Through the look
Of her inner eye
That she feeds
His want
And in her song
She brings him
Into the mountains
Of what matters.

Because of her voice
She elevates
His being
From outliving self
To epiphany
And he feels
The power
Of her presence
The power
Of inspiration.

He is driven
To please her
And in return
She offers him
Visions
Into the unknown.

How
Truth within hidden
Meaning
That she nourishes him
Throttles his seeing
As mind throbs
Through being in time.

How
The sound of her voice
Grabs his being.

So
He finds
In her voice
The passion
Of being toward Truth.

*

Venturing
Into the advent
Of the unknown
The artist
Carves the face
Of being
As cosmic consciousness
Invites the artist
To the domain
Of the absolutes.

Surrounded
By the possible
He leaps
Into a portal
To hidden meaning
And the barriers
Of the concealed
Collapse.

Before Truth
There is no mask
And the muse

Shines light
On the other.

Together
They frame the beauty
Of the always
Already there
And mind bleeds
With Truth.

How
The moment
Occupies the dwelling
Of the in-most parts
Where being toward Truth
Defines
What matters.

It is
In the voice
Of the muse
That the artist
Harvests treasures
And the other
Touches
Phenomenal reality.

Then
Assumption is

Left behind.

*

So
A man and a woman
Strolled
By the river side
And earth tones
Dominated the moment.

No one was there
Except the two
And the artist
With his inner eye
As a cloudy sky
Filtered the light.

They were the center
Of the universe
As mind configured them
Into a parabola of time.

Then
The celestial clocks
Pulled them to the edge
Of nothingness
And the muse spoke
Meaning into being toward Truth.

As the artist
Plunged
Int6o deep trance
The man and woman
Walked alone
Discussing where
They would go
From there.

They were
Concealed by the moment
But the muse
Allowed
The artist to witness
Their time.

How
Powerful this thing
Called love
When nothingness attempts
To empty all
Into the void.

Although time passed
The artist connected
To their moment
And he became
The other.

*

In the grammar
Of being toward Truth
The language
Of cosmic consciousness
Emanates
Through the inner eye.

Here
The beginning of ideation
Touches the artist
As the muse
Speaks
The passion
Of being toward Truth
Into the moment.

How
The artist records
The time
With the connectivity
Of love
As the muse
Nurtures mind.

There is
The history
Of times and a half
When the artist
Bled pain
Because the muse
Was not there.

Then
When she returned
The artist found
Life
Pounding in his chest
And the muse
Honored his need.

How
The river of beauty
Connects them
In moments of wonder
As wave upon wave
Of her waters
Flows
Into his being.

So
Now he beholds
The cosmic consciousness.

*

It was
Dawn when the artist
Awoke
With the voice
Of the muse in mind
And it filled him
With the desire
For Truth.

Opening his eyes
To the given
He saw
Through the expanse
Of time and space
As the authentic article
Slipped into view.

So
The moon appeared
Full and round
In the west
And the muse
Unearthed the secrets
Of hidden meaning.

It was
In his dreams
That she occupied
His mind
Turning image after image
And the artist heard
Her voice
Through it all.

So
Truth is where
Being touches
Nothingness
When pain and suffering
And outliving the self

Become the past.

Then
The now
Of being toward Truth takes
The artist
Into the heart
Of the muse
As they join
The flight of crows
The free spirits.

So
Truth is on the wing.

*

So
What is a free spirit
If not
The flight
Of the crystal crow.

How
They belong to the sky
And times beyond the sky.

It is
That their heart
Is fastened
To the celestial clocks

As the cosmic
Consciousness
Allows them liberty.

Then
They approach
A vertical column of time
Finding their way
To what matters.

They are
The magi of always
And forever
On a mission
To sustain life
Calling upon destiny
To give them
A place
In the always
Already there.

Time speaks
A language
Coming from the bones
Of being toward Truth
And liberty
Is a call to life.

So
The muse
Joins their flight

Carrying the artist
To visions of eternity
And the anthems
Of forevermore
Trumpet
In their blood.

Freedom
Is their birthright.

*

A hooded figure
Dark and foreboding
Faces being toward Truth
From the shadows
Holding a skull
In two cupped hands.

Pain flows
From the image
A savage attack
As wave upon wave
Pounds away at mind.

Then
The artist
Looks for light
Bu only a shroud
Of darkness
Fills the space.

Then
The crystal crown enters time
The crystal crown of thorns
Glowing
Ever so brightly.

It is
Of shinning gold.

How
Out of the unknown
Comes hope
As free spirits
Choose
A direction of coming
And ripples
Of thunder crease
Times and a half.

It is
In a parabola of time
That the image
Shifts
And mercy flourishes
In the beating heart.

Then
In the eye sockets
Of the skull
Candles flicker
As faith

Carries the moment.

*

As church bells
Chime the hour
Time and space carry
The artist
Into the unknown.

There is
An agony
In his bones
As he looks
To the muse
And she
Directs him
To The Counselor
The Spirit of Truth.

How
Those of the tormented
Dwell
In a house of horrors
Begging for deliverance
And there is
Hope
In The Word.

As being toward Truth
Submits

To wehat seems
Like destiny
The artist sees
A beacon shining through his misery.

Then
He is on a voyage
Guided
By The Word
As his faith
In The Unknown God
Releases the bond
Of chains
And his mind
Is no longer haunted.

As his ship
Is righted
He leaves his misery
And sails
Into the sun rise.

His true destiny speaks of hope.

To dwell
In the good
The right practice.

*

Among the mountains
Of wilderness
The artist searches
For hidden meaning
As the sky
Opens what matters.

A tension fills the air
As times elude
The present.

Then
The muse infuses
Being toward Truth
With the authentic
Article
And the artist
Sketches the other
As a kindred spirit.

There is
A connection
Of minds
Where cosmic consciousness
Allows
Becoming free spirits
And crows launch
Truth.

Then
The substance

Of the concealed
Surfaces
Its form part
Of the close at hand.

To grasp
The awakening
Of ideation
How
The muse energizes
The artist
And his vision stirs.

In the wilderness
One flower blooms
And it is
The hidden meaning
In being toward Truth.

*

Leaving the body
Behind
The artist ventured
Into the unknown
Hoping to unearth
What mattered.

By himself
He advanced
Through a portal

That led his mind
Beyond the here and now.

The close at hand
Melted
Into negative space
As he saw
The crystal crow headed
Toward forevermore.

There was
A message encrypted
In the moment
As the muse
Lifted
A horizon of Truth
Into view
Revealing times
And times and a half.

Then
The moment released
The form
Of being toward Truth
And the muse
Connected the artist
To cosmic consciousness.

As being in time
Unfolded
In the beginning of ideation

The muse defined
An image
Of the other
With a face
Wearing a mask
And it dangled there.

So
Truth wears a mask
Before the here
And now.

So
Being toward Truth
Uncovers Truth
In the call
Of what matters most.